The Future of YouTube: Leveraging AI for Unbeatable Content and Account Management

Chapter 1
Understanding AI Basics

Artificial Intelligence (AI) is a revolutionary field that empowers machines to mimic human intelligence and perform tasks that typically require human cognitive abilities. In simple terms, AI is all about creating computer systems capable of learning, reasoning, and making decisions. This chapter delves into the various applications of AI across different industries, such as healthcare, finance, transportation, and entertainment. From autonomous vehicles to virtual assistants, AI is transforming the way we live, work, and interact with technology.

To better understand the current state of AI, it is crucial to explore its historical progression. This section takes a journey through the milestones and breakthroughs that have shaped AI over the years. From the early days of symbolic AI and expert systems to the emergence of machine learning and neural networks, we trace the path that has led us to the AI renaissance we witness today. By understanding the challenges and successes of the past, we can gain valuable insights into the future of AI.

As with any specialized field, AI comes with its own set of concepts and terminology. This section introduces essential terms and ideas that form the foundation of AI understanding. From algorithms to data preprocessing, from reinforcement learning to unsupervised learning, we cover the fundamental knowledge necessary to navigate the world of AI. By mastering these concepts, readers will be equipped with the vocabulary and understanding they need to fully grasp the subsequent chapters and harness the power of AI.

Machine learning is a subset of AI that focuses on developing algorithms that can learn from data and make predictions or decisions without explicit programming. In this chapter, we explore the different types of machine learning algorithms, such as supervised learning, unsupervised learning, and reinforcement learning. We dive into the mathematical principles that underlie these algorithms and explore real-life examples to illustrate their effectiveness. By the end of this chapter, readers will have a solid grasp of the core principles of machine learning.

Deep learning, a subfield of machine learning, has gained significant attention in recent years for its remarkable performance in tasks such as image recognition and natural language processing. At the heart of deep learning are neural networks, computational models inspired by the human brain. This section delves into the structure and functioning of neural networks, explaining layers, neurons, and activation functions. We also explore specific types of neural networks, such as convolutional neural networks for image analysis and recurrent neural networks for sequential data processing.

Language is a fundamental mode of communication, and AI has made tremendous strides in understanding and processing it. This section introduces natural language processing (NLP), a branch of AI dedicated to analyzing and generating human language. We delve into sentiment analysis, a technique that extracts emotions and opinions from text, as well as language generation, which involves generating human-like text. Additionally, we explore voice recognition and speech-to-text technologies, which enable AI systems to understand and transcribe spoken language.

Computer vision is an interdisciplinary field that combines AI, image processing, and pattern recognition to enable machines to understand and interpret visual information. In this chapter, we explore the applications of computer vision in AI, ranging from object detection to image and video segmentation. We dive into state-of-the-art algorithms and techniques used in computer vision, such as convolutional neural networks and feature extraction. Understanding computer vision is crucial for leveraging AI in areas such as autonomous vehicles, surveillance systems, and image recognition.

Data plays a pivotal role in AI development and improvement. This chapter explores the importance of data in training AI models and the challenges and opportunities associated with big data analysis. We delve into the techniques of data mining, which involve extracting patterns and knowledge from large datasets. By harnessing the power of big data, AI systems can uncover valuable insights and make informed decisions. Understanding data mining and big data analytics is essential for professionals seeking to leverage AI for data-driven decision-making.

While AI offers immense potential, it also raises ethical concerns. In this chapter, we explore the issues surrounding bias and fairness in AI systems. We delve into topics such as algorithmic transparency, accountability, and explainability. Moreover, we discuss the importance of addressing these ethical considerations and implementing responsible AI practices. By understanding these challenges, readers will be equipped to navigate the ethical landscape of AI and ensure the responsible use of this powerful technology.

The field of AI is ever-evolving, with new advancements and trends constantly emerging. In this chapter, we explore the potential impact of emerging AI technologies on various industries. We discuss recent innovations in computer vision, natural language processing, and other areas of AI. Furthermore, we examine the possibilities of AI in fields such as healthcare, education, and entertainment. By staying informed about the latest trends and innovations, readers will be prepared for the future of AI and its potential applications.

Chapter 2
Setting Up Your AI-Enabled YouTube Studio

YouTube content creation has been revolutionized by the integration of artificial intelligence (AI). This chapter explores the impact of AI on various aspects of YouTube content creation, revealing its immense potential in enhancing efficiency and creativity.

AI algorithms have transformed video editing and production processes, enabling creators to produce high-quality content with ease. By leveraging AI-powered tools and software, creators can automate mundane tasks like video trimming, color correction, and transition effects. This not only saves time but also ensures consistent visual aesthetics throughout the video.

Furthermore, AI assists in content ideation and recommendation by analyzing user engagement patterns and preferences. AI algorithms can process large amounts of data to identify trends, topics, and formats that resonate with the audience. Creators can then use these insights to craft engaging content that appeals to their target viewers.

Developing an efficient production workflow is crucial for content creators on YouTube.By integrating AI in video editing and post-production processes, creators can unlock new possibilities for creativity. AI-powered software can automatically sync audio and video, detect and remove background noise, and even suggest optimal shot compositions. These tools empower creators to focus on the artistic aspects of their content, while AI takes care of the technicalities.

Moreover, creators can enhance their production workflow by investing in AI-enabled hardware solutions. These include powerful processors, specialized graphics cards, and machine learning accelerators. By selecting the right AI hardware, creators can achieve faster rendering times, seamless multitasking, and improved real-time editing capabilities.

The availability of various AI tools and software can be overwhelming for content creators. This section provides an overview of different AI tools and helps creators make informed decisions on selecting the most suitable ones for their YouTube studio.

Understanding the different AI tools available for content creation is essential. From facial recognition for automatic tagging to sentiment analysis for understanding viewer emotions, these tools offer a wide range of functionalities. Creators can leverage AI tools for video editing, metadata generation, content optimization, and more.

When evaluating AI software options for video editing and optimization, creators should consider factors such as user-friendliness, compatibility, and support services. User reviews and expert recommendations can provide valuable insights into the performance and reliability of different AI software options.

Additionally, creators should choose AI-enabled hardware that complements their software requirements. High-performance graphics cards, sufficient RAM, and efficient cooling systems are some essential considerations. By selecting the right combination of software and hardware, creators can maximize the capabilities of their AI-enabled YouTube studios.

Personalizing content stands as a cornerstone in captivating and engaging viewers. Today, the spotlight falls on creators leveraging machine learning to train AI models, fostering a rich environment for personalized content creation.

Machine learning, a tool of unparalleled potential, facilitates a nuanced understanding of audience preferences and trends. Creators harness this technology to glean insights into viewers' interests and behavior, setting a stage for content that resonates profoundly with various audience segments. Techniques such as clustering and recommendation systems come into play, allowing for a segmentation of the audience into distinct groups, each receiving content tailored to their preferences.

A critical phase in this endeavor is the collection and processing of data, a step that empowers AI models to craft personalized content. Analytics tools serve as vital instruments in this process, gathering data on viewer interactions, watch time, and engagement metrics. These data points, rich with information, become the training ground for AI models, guiding them to predict viewer preferences and sculpt personalized content recommendations.

Dynamic content creation emerges as a powerful strategy, one rooted in real-time viewer interaction and feedback. AI algorithms stand ready to adjust video content automatically, responding to real-time feedback such as likes, dislikes, comments, and shares. This iterative process nurtures a deeper bond between creators and their audience, paving the way for heightened engagement and loyalty.

Creators find themselves at a juncture where innovation meets tradition, where AI not only predicts but also responds to viewer preferences, crafting content that is both fresh and resonant. The journey is one of learning and adaptation, a continuous cycle of feedback and refinement, fostering a community where every viewer finds content that speaks to them, that understands them, and that brings them back, time and again.

In this emerging realm of AI, case studies stand as testimony to the success achievable through machine learning. They offer a glimpse into the journeys of YouTube creators who have navigated this path with skill and foresight, leveraging machine learning to craft content that is not just viewed but cherished.

As we stand on the threshold of a future rich with potential, creators hold the key to a world of content that is as diverse as it is personalized. Armed with the knowledge and tools detailed in this section, creators are not just prepared but empowered to forge paths that resonate with authenticity and innovation, ushering in a new era of personalized content creation on YouTube, a space where every viewer feels seen, heard, and valued.

Chapter 3
AI for Content Strategy

Lets next take a look at how content strategy plays a crucial role in capturing and retaining the attention of online audiences. As users consume vast amounts of content across various platforms, the need to deliver personalized and engaging experiences has never been greater. This is where Artificial Intelligence (AI) emerges as a powerful tool for content creators and strategists. In this chapter, we will explore how AI can transform content strategy by enhancing audience analysis, enabling content personalization, automating content creation and curation, optimizing content distribution, measuring content performance, aiding content planning and ideation, facilitating content localization and global reach, and addressing ethical considerations. By understanding the potential benefits and challenges of AI-driven content strategy, creators can harness this technology to thrive in the digital landscape.

The evolution of content strategy in the digital age:

Today, content strategy has evolved beyond the traditional methods of storytelling and brand positioning. With the proliferation of digital platforms and the exponential growth of content, strategists must navigate a complex landscape to captivate audiences effectively. AI offers the potential to revolutionize content strategy by providing data-driven insights and automating processes that were once time-consuming and resource-intensive.

How AI can enhance and optimize content strategy:

AI technologies, such as machine learning and natural language processing, enable content strategists to analyze vast amounts of data quickly and accurately. By understanding audience preferences, sentiment, and behavior, AI can help determine the type of content that resonates with viewers. Additionally, AI-powered tools aid in optimizing content distribution, recommendations, and personalization, maximizing the reach and impact of content.

Exploring the benefits and challenges of AI-driven content strategy:

The benefits of AI-driven content strategy are numerous. AI can improve audience engagement, drive content performance, enhance creativity, and enable efficient decision-making. However, implementing AI in content strategy comes with challenges. Ethical concerns, algorithmic biases, and the need for data privacy and security are areas that content creators and strategists must navigate carefully. By understanding the potential risks and proactively addressing them, creators can leverage AI to its fullest potential.

AI-powered algorithms can process large volumes of data to reveal valuable insights about audience demographics and preferences. By analyzing user behavior, engagement metrics, and other data points, content strategists can gain a deeper understanding of their target audience. This knowledge allows them to create content that aligns with audience expectations, interests, and needs.

Identifying trends and patterns in viewer behavior with AI:

AI algorithms excel at identifying trends, patterns, and correlations within datasets. By leveraging machine learning techniques, content strategists can uncover hidden insights from viewer interactions, preferences, and engagement metrics. Understanding these trends enables strategists to predict emerging topics, anticipate shifts in audience interests, and tailor content accordingly.

Incorporating AI-driven audience insights into content strategy:

AI-driven audience insights provide content strategists with a competitive edge. By integrating these insights into content strategy, creators can align their content with audience preferences, optimize content distribution channels, and deliver personalized experiences. Through continuous analysis and refinement, AI-powered audience insights foster an iterative and data-driven approach to content strategy development.

The power of AI in delivering personalized content experiences:

Personalization is key to engaging audiences in an increasingly crowded digital landscape. AI empowers content creators to deliver personalized content experiences by leveraging user data and preferences. Machine learning algorithms can analyze user interactions, past behavior, and contextual data to tailor content recommendations and create customized experiences.

Utilizing AI algorithms for targeted content recommendations:

AI algorithms enable content platforms to recommend relevant content to users based on their preferences and viewing history. By leveraging machine learning models, creators can deliver highly targeted recommendations that align with individual viewer's interests, increasing engagement and time spent on their platforms. This personalization also fosters a deeper connection between creators and their audience.

Customizing content based on viewer preferences and interests:

AI can assist creators in customizing content to individual viewer preferences and interests. By analyzing data on viewer interactions and feedback, content strategists can better understand the specific needs and expectations of their audience. With this knowledge, creators can adapt their content to better resonate with viewers, ensuring a personalized and engaging experience.

AI-powered tools and algorithms can automate various aspects of content creation, enhancing efficiency and creativity. This automation revolutionizes the creative process, streamlining workflows and optimizing resource allocation. Tasks that once consumed substantial time and energy, such as video trimming, color correction, and crafting transition effects, now find themselves in the capable hands of AI, allowing creators to channel their focus toward the artistic nuances of their content.

The role of AI extends to the pivotal task of content curation. Leveraging machine learning algorithms, creators can sift through vast data sources swiftly, selecting content that perfectly aligns with their audience's preferences. AI stands as a powerful ally in identifying emerging trends and popular topics, offering creators a rich palette of engaging formats from which to craft compelling narratives.

AI's influence doen't end at automation and curation; it breathes new life into the creative process itself. AI technologies open up avenues of creativity previously unimagined, encouraging creators to experiment with new formats, styles, and ideas. By taking on the repetitive tasks, AI frees creators to venture beyond the conventional boundaries, to craft content that is not just watched but experienced, fostering a deeper connection with the audience.

As creators venture into this dynamic ecosystem, they find a space brimming with opportunities to push the boundaries of what is possible. The collaboration between AI and creators fosters a symbiotic relationship, a partnership where technology meets creativity, offering a canvas of unlimited potential. It is a dance of possibilities, where the tools and insights provided by AI merge seamlessly with the vision and artistry of creators, crafting narratives that are compelling, authentic, and deeply resonant.

Looking forward, we envision a world where AI is not just a tool but a collaborator in the truest sense, a partner in the journey of content creation. It is a future where narratives are crafted with a deep understanding of the audience's pulse, where content is not just created but sculpted to resonate on a profound level, offering viewers experiences that are rich, immersive, and deeply personal.

In this era of AI-driven content creation and curation, creators stand as visionaries, leveraging the power of AI to craft masterpieces that speak to the heart of the audience. It is a journey of discovery, a path of innovation, and a testament to the boundless potential of human creativity, enhanced and elevated by the power of AI technology. It is a journey we embark on with anticipation, ready to redefine the landscape of content creation, one AI-powered step at a time.

Chapter 4
Smart Editing with AI

In recent years, the video editing sector has undergone a significant transformation, largely propelled by the advent of Artificial Intelligence (AI). This chapter sheds light on the revolutionary changes AI has brought to video editing, emphasizing the advancements in AI-powered tools and the myriad of benefits they offer to YouTube creators and the broader content creation industry.

Artificial Intelligence has ushered in a new era in video editing, making the process more streamlined and accessible to creators at various levels. AI-powered tools have taken over the laborious tasks of scene detection, trimming, and applying visual effects, freeing creators to focus more on the creative nuances of their content. Machine learning algorithms have introduced the concept of real-time editing, a development that has enhanced viewer engagement and opened up a plethora of creative avenues.

In this dynamic environment, AI-powered video editing tools and software have seen remarkable advancements. These tools, armed with deep learning and computer vision algorithms, analyze and process video data with unprecedented efficiency. They offer features such as automatic scene detection, intelligent trimming, and visual effects recommendations, integrating seamlessly with existing workflows and enhancing productivity. The user-friendly interfaces of these tools have been a game-changer, making the editing process not just efficient but also enjoyable.

One notable tool in this sphere is Runway, which leverages AI to offer a range of video editing features, including object removal and style transfer, allowing creators to modify the visual style of their videos easily. Another tool, Magisto, uses AI to analyze and edit videos automatically, identifying the most interesting parts of a video and editing them together with music and effects to match the mood. Tools like these have transformed the editing process, making it faster and more intuitive.

AI-driven smart editing has proven to be a boon for YouTube creators, offering a range of benefits. It saves time and effort by automating repetitive editing tasks, allowing for a more efficient content production process. Moreover, AI can enhance video aesthetics significantly by recommending and applying visual effects that align perfectly with the desired style and tone of the content. The real-time video editing techniques powered by AI have enabled creators to engage viewers dynamically, capturing their attention and providing a rich viewing experience.

AI algorithms are at the heart of automatic video editing techniques. Leveraging machine learning and computer vision, these algorithms meticulously analyze video content, identifying scenes, detecting objects, and recognizing patterns. Trained with vast amounts of data, they automate tasks such as scene detection, framing, object removal, and video stabilization, ensuring consistent and visually appealing results.

Scene detection is a pivotal aspect of video editing, helping creators identify and separate different shots or scenes within a video seamlessly. AI-powered machine learning algorithms can automatically analyze frames to detect transitions, such as cuts or dissolves, and segment the video accordingly. Trimming, a process that involves removing unnecessary or redundant footage, can also be automated using machine learning algorithms, which analyze patterns and viewer engagement to suggest optimal trimming points, improving the overall flow and pacing of the video.

Visual effects are vital in enhancing the overall aesthetics and impact of a video. AI-driven algorithms can analyze the content and context of a video to recommend suitable visual effects, such as color grading, filter application, and motion graphics. These algorithms learn from existing aesthetic preferences and trends, enabling creators to achieve visually stunning and cohesive results, enhancing the overall quality and appeal of the video content.

Integration of AI tools into the video editing workflow has been a game-changer, enhancing efficiency and productivity. These tools offer functionalities like automated file management, real-time collaboration, and cloud-based storage, streamlining the overall workflow and saving time for creators to focus on the creative aspects of content creation.

Traditionally, video editing involved several repetitive tasks, such as file organization, transcoding, and clip alignment. AI has automated these tasks, saving time for creators to devote more energy to the artistic and storytelling aspects of their content. It handles file naming conventions, detects and converts file formats, and aligns clips based on visual similarities, eliminating the need for manual intervention.

AI-driven video editing has enhanced efficiency and productivity by automating time-consuming tasks and providing intelligent recommendations. It enables creators to work seamlessly across different platforms and devices, facilitating collaboration and improving overall productivity. By harnessing the power of AI, creators can achieve faster and more streamlined video editing workflows, optimizing the editing process based on data on viewer engagement, preferences, and trending topics.

Content recommendation systems have been revolutionized by AI algorithms, playing a crucial role in driving viewer engagement and retention. By analyzing user data, preferences, and viewing patterns, AI tools can recommend relevant content within videos, improving the viewer experience and leading to increased viewer engagement, longer watch times, and improved content discoverability.

AI enhances the viewer experience by providing intelligent content enhancement, automatically adjusting lighting, color grading, and exposure levels to improve the visual quality of videos. It can also enhance audio quality by reducing background noise, improving clarity, and normalizing volume levels, resulting in a more immersive and enjoyable viewing experience for the audience.

AI enables content customization by analyzing viewer preferences and interests, creating user profiles based on data such as watch history, search queries, and engagement metrics. This allows creators to deliver personalized content suggestions tailored to individual viewer preferences, improving viewer satisfaction and strengthening the bond between creators and their audience.

Chapter 5
SEO Optimization with AI

In the dynamic sphere of YouTube, a platform teeming with creativity and a plethora of content, standing out necessitates more than just crafting high-quality videos. The pivotal role of Search Engine Optimization (SEO) comes to the fore, steering the helm in the vast ocean of content, guiding creators to the shores of visibility and organic traffic. This chapter unveils the potent synergy of SEO and Artificial Intelligence (AI), a collaboration that promises to redefine the paradigms of content discoverability on YouTube, offering creators a roadmap to success in a space where competition is fierce and unyielding.

Today, the digital canvas is vibrant, ever-changing, and demands a strategy that is both robust and adaptive. SEO stands tall as a beacon, ensuring that the labor of love and creativity finds its way to the right audience, an audience that appreciates and engages with the content. It is not just about creating; it is about being seen, being heard, and connecting with viewers who resonate with the creator's vision. SEO is the silent architect behind a YouTube channel's visibility, meticulously crafting pathways that increase the likelihood of appearing in search results, thereby driving a steady stream of organic traffic to the content. Moreover, SEO fine-tunes the user experience, presenting viewers with content that is not just relevant but finely aligned with their preferences, fostering a space where content and viewer harmoniously coexist.

As we navigate further, we find that SEO wields a significant influence on video rankings in search engine results pages, a factor that directly correlates with visibility and organic traffic. The meticulous optimization of various elements such as metadata, titles, descriptions, and tags with pertinent keywords can elevate videos to higher ranking positions. This strategy not only augments visibility but fosters a rich ground for organic traffic, culminating in a surge in views, watch time, and engagement. Furthermore, SEO serves as a magnet, attracting an audience that is genuinely interested and likely to engage with the content, creating a win-win situation for both creators and viewers.

In this vibrant ecosystem, AI emerges as a powerful ally, offering tools and algorithms that significantly enhance SEO optimization on YouTube. It facilitates a nuanced approach to keyword research and analysis, helping creators pinpoint high-ranking keywords that resonate profoundly with their target audience. But the role of AI is not confined to keywords; it extends to enhancing video titles, descriptions, and tags, thereby maximizing content visibility. Moreover, AI-driven content optimization techniques coupled with intelligent video analytics empower creators to make informed, data-driven decisions, fine-tuning their SEO strategies for optimum results.

In the vast ocean of data, AI algorithms stand as lighthouses, guiding creators to the most relevant and high-ranking keywords that align perfectly with their content narrative. These powerful algorithms analyze search queries, user behavior, and trending topics, recommending keywords that hold the golden ticket to optimal SEO performance. The right keywords become the bridge connecting creators with their potential audience, paving the way for improved organic search visibility.

AI tools are equipped with functionalities that go beyond mere keyword suggestions; they offer a deep analysis of search volume, competition level, and keyword trends, providing creators with a rich tapestry of insights. These insights, derived from machine learning and natural language processing, understand user intent at a granular level, recommending keywords that echo the search queries of the target audience. This intelligent optimization of video titles, descriptions, and tags ensures a harmonious alignment with viewer expectations, fostering a content-viewer synergy that is both organic and rewarding.

As we steer towards the conclusion of this part, we understand that AI is not just a tool; it is a collaborator, a partner in the creative journey, offering insights that are both deep and actionable. It analyzes vast arrays of data, offering a roadmap to creators, a roadmap that promises visibility and engagement. AI stands as a testament to the advancements in technology, a tool that promises to redefine the paradigms of SEO optimization on YouTube, offering a canvas where creativity meets technology, a space where content is not just created but celebrated.

In this part of the chapter, we have navigated the vibrant and dynamic space of YouTube SEO optimization, understanding the pivotal role of SEO and the transformative potential of AI in enhancing content discoverability. As we move forward, we will delve deeper, unveiling the multifaceted role of AI in SEO optimization, a journey that promises to be both enlightening and empowering for YouTube creators. Let us forge ahead, with AI as our ally, in this journey of discovery and success in the competitive yet exhilarating space of YouTube.

In the vibrant and ever-evolving YouTube ecosystem, the role of AI-driven insights in optimizing video titles, descriptions, and tags cannot be overstated. Creators are now equipped with tools that facilitate intelligent optimization, allowing them to align their content seamlessly with the interests and preferences of their target audience. The integration of high-ranking keywords, derived from a meticulous analysis of search volumes, user engagement, and competition, empowers creators to craft metadata that not only enhances SEO performance but also beckons organic traffic, setting a stage for a rich and engaging viewer experience.

As we venture further, we find that AI algorithms stand as powerful allies in optimizing video content for search relevance. These algorithms delve into the rich tapestry of user behavior, historical data, and content trends, offering creators a goldmine of insights into viewer preferences and interests. Leveraging these insights allows creators to tailor their content meticulously, aligning it perfectly with the search intent of the target audience. The recommendations offered by AI, be it incorporating specific topics, formats, or visual elements, serve to enhance search relevance, promising a rich and rewarding SEO performance.

In this dynamic space, the role of AI tools extends to automatic content tagging and categorization, a process pivotal to SEO optimization. These tools, equipped with image and video recognition capabilities, undertake the task of tagging and categorizing video content based on visual features and context. This intelligent labeling of videos not only enhances searchability and discoverability but promises a consistency and accuracy in metadata, a feature that stands central to a successful SEO strategy.

As we navigate this intricate landscape, we witness the transformative potential of AI-driven optimization strategies in enhancing video metadata. These strategies, grounded in a deep analysis of search trends, user behavior, and content similarities, offer creators a roadmap to improving metadata quality. AI tools stand as collaborators in this journey, recommending the most engaging thumbnail images, crafting compelling titles, and formulating informative descriptions that resonate profoundly with search intent. This strategy promises not just enhanced discoverability but a surge in click-through rates, setting a stage for a rich and engaging viewer experience.

In the competitive space of YouTube, thumbnails hold a pivotal role, serving as the first point of contact between the content and the viewer. AI algorithms, with their powerful image recognition capabilities, assist creators in crafting thumbnails that are not just visually appealing but hold a high engagement potential. These algorithms analyze video content meticulously, identifying key visual elements and exciting frames, promising thumbnails that beckon viewers, encouraging them to engage with the content.

As we forge ahead, we find that AI algorithms hold the key to thumbnail optimization and A/B testing, a strategy that promises to increase the effectiveness of thumbnails manifold. Leveraging machine learning models and A/B testing, creators can identify the most engaging thumbnail variations, a strategy grounded in a deep analysis of viewer behavior and visual preferences. This systematic testing of different thumbnail designs allows creators to refine their approach, selecting thumbnails that resonate profoundly with the target audience, promising maximized viewer engagement.

In this journey of optimization, AI-powered thumbnails emerge as powerful tools in enhancing viewer engagement and click-through rates. These thumbnails, crafted with a deep understanding of viewer preferences, convey the video's content effectively, promising to stand out in search results. The strategy, grounded in the use of eye-catching visuals and compelling imagery, increases the likelihood of viewers choosing to engage with the video, setting a stage for a rich and rewarding viewer experience.

As we steer towards the conclusion of this chapter, we delve into the potent synergy of AI-driven video transcription in improving accessibility and SEO. AI technology, with its advanced speech recognition capabilities, promises accurate and efficient video transcriptions, a feature that ensures content accessibility to viewers with hearing impairments and language barriers. This strategy not only enhances SEO but promises improved search visibility and organic traffic, fostering a space where content is accessible and engaging.

In this vibrant ecosystem, the role of closed captions emerges as pivotal, serving to enhance video discoverability while promising improved accessibility. Leveraging AI-powered tools allows creators to craft accurate closed captions, a strategy grounded in speech recognition and natural language processing algorithms. This approach not only makes content accessible to a wider audience but promises improved discoverability, increasing the potential audience reach manifold.

As we conclude this chapter, we witness the transformative potential of AI in multilingual transcription and captioning, a strategy that promises to overcome language barriers and reach global audiences. Leveraging machine learning algorithms allows creators to transcribe and caption videos in multiple languages accurately, a feature that not only improves accessibility but broadens content reach and appeal. This strategy promises to attract viewers from diverse linguistic backgrounds, fostering a space where engagement is rich and the content reach is truly international.

In this chapter, we have navigated the vibrant and dynamic space of YouTube SEO optimization, understanding the pivotal role of SEO and the transformative potential of AI in enhancing content discoverability. As we forge ahead in this journey of content creation, AI stands as a powerful ally, promising a canvas where creativity meets technology, a space where content is not just created but celebrated. Let us embrace this potent synergy of AI and SEO, as we craft content that is not just visible but truly resonant, setting a stage for a rich and rewarding YouTube journey.

Chapter 6
Creating Personalized Viewer Experiences

Understanding that personalization stands as a vital tool in the toolkit of a YouTube creator is essential. Leveraging AI technologies not only aids in tailoring content to meet individual preferences but also fosters a more connected and engaging viewer experience. This chapter will elucidate the various strategies and AI tools available for YouTube creators to enhance personalization, helping them to craft content that resonates with individual tastes and preferences.

Understanding your audience is a critical step in creating content that resonates. AI offers potent tools that analyze complex viewership data, providing insights into the diverse viewer base and aiding creators in developing content that appeals to different segments. Audience segmentation, which involves categorizing the audience into distinct groups based on various criteria such as demographics and viewing patterns, allows creators to design content that fosters deeper connections with viewers. By understanding the nuances of their audience's preferences, creators can tailor their content strategies to meet the specific needs and interests of different viewer groups, enhancing viewer satisfaction and building a loyal audience.

AI algorithms play a critical role in analyzing viewer interactions to suggest content that is more likely to be appreciated, thereby fostering increased engagement and viewer satisfaction. These algorithms work by analyzing data such as viewing history, likes, and comments to understand viewer preferences and suggest content that aligns with their interests. This not only helps in keeping the viewers engaged but also in discovering new content that they might enjoy, creating a more personalized and satisfying viewing experience.

Dynamic content generation is another area where AI can make a significant impact. This involves the automated creation of content elements such as intros and outros based on real-time viewer input, offering a unique and tailored viewing experience. For instance, AI can be used to create personalized video overlays that change based on the viewer's preferences, creating a dynamic and interactive viewing experience that stands out.

Interactive elements, including quizzes and polls, have seen a surge in popularity. Enhanced through AI, these elements offer a more immersive viewing experience, encouraging viewers to actively participate and engage with the content. Creators can use AI to analyze the responses to these interactive elements, gaining valuable insights into their audience's preferences and tailoring their content strategies accordingly.

AI technologies can optimize video recommendations, encouraging viewers to explore more content on your channel, thus fostering sustained engagement and a deeper connection with the audience. Personalized playlists, created based on AI analysis of viewer preferences, can foster viewer loyalty by offering content tailored to individual preferences, encouraging repeated visits and fostering a community of dedicated viewers.

Chatbots and voice assistants powered by AI can assist creators in real-time engagement with their audience, answering queries and recommending relevant content, thereby fostering a vibrant and interactive community. These tools can be programmed to provide instant responses to common viewer queries, offering real-time assistance and fostering a sense of community and engagement.

Gamification involves incorporating game-like elements such as rewards and challenges into videos to enhance viewer engagement. AI can facilitate gamification by helping creators design interactive challenges and reward systems that encourage viewers to engage more deeply with the content, fostering a sense of community and encouraging sharing and repeated engagement.

In the realm of personalization, it is crucial to address the ethical considerations surrounding the use of viewer data. Creators must respect viewer privacy and employ data responsibly, adopting strategies such as obtaining consent and ensuring secure data storage to foster trust and safeguard viewer privacy.

Looking forward, emerging trends in AI, including hyper-personalization and augmented reality, hold immense potential to revolutionize YouTube content creation. By staying abreast of the latest developments in AI, creators can maintain a competitive edge in the dynamic landscape of YouTube, offering content that is not only engaging but also at the forefront of technological advancements.

In conclusion, personalization stands as a pivotal tool in attracting and retaining viewers on YouTube, fostering deeper connections and a vibrant community. By leveraging AI technologies, creators can foster deeper connections with their audience and drive long-term growth on the YouTube platform, encouraging creators to embrace these technologies in their content creation strategies.

Chapter 7
Automated Account Management

In the ever-evolving ecosystem of YouTube, creators are constantly seeking innovative solutions to streamline their processes and enhance the reach and impact of their content. Automated account management, powered by the latest advancements in artificial intelligence, emerges as a pivotal tool in this endeavor, offering a plethora of benefits that range from optimizing content scheduling to fostering a positive and inclusive community environment.

Automation has become an indispensable ally in managing YouTube accounts with a heightened level of efficiency and effectiveness. By incorporating automated processes in various facets of account management, creators find themselves with the luxury of time, which can be channeled into crafting high-quality content. The role of automation extends to analytics tracking, a critical aspect that provides a deep understanding of viewer engagement and opens avenues for optimizing content strategies.

As we delve further into the intricacies of automation, we find AI-powered tools revolutionizing content scheduling and publishing, offering creators a golden opportunity to plan and automate their video release strategies meticulously. By analyzing viewer behaviors and optimizing posting times, these tools ensure videos receive maximum exposure, enhancing audience reach and engagement significantly. The AI doesn't stop there; it extends its prowess to video metadata optimization, a critical process in improving search engine visibility and driving organic traffic to YouTube content. Leveraging AI-based tools for keyword research, tag generation, and title optimization, creators can significantly increase their videos' discoverability, attracting a larger audience in the process.

Community engagement stands as a pillar in building a successful YouTube channel, and managing comments effectively can often be a time-consuming task. Here, AI algorithms come to the rescue, offering automation in comment moderation and spam detection, ensuring a positive and inclusive environment for the community while freeing creators to focus on other vital tasks. Moreover, AI technologies offer a helping hand in channel growth and monetization strategies, providing actionable recommendations derived from a detailed analysis of audience demographics, content engagement, and revenue trends.

In the dynamic YouTube ecosystem, promoting content across social media platforms is no small feat. AI-powered tools step in, automating social media scheduling and content sharing, thereby expanding audience reach and increasing brand visibility substantially. These tools also facilitate cross-platform integration, driving substantial traffic to the YouTube channel and fostering growth.

A crucial element that often serves as the first point of contact between the viewer and the content is the thumbnail. AI comes into play here, automating thumbnail generation and performing A/B testing to identify the most compelling designs, optimizing visual appeal, and maximizing video discoverability. Furthermore, AI technologies such as Content ID stand as guardians in protecting copyrighted content, enabling creators to maintain a fair and lawful presence on the platform.

As we steer towards the horizon, we see the future holding immense potential with advancements in AI technologies. Emerging trends like predictive analytics and machine learning are set to redefine the paradigms of automated account management, offering YouTube creators unprecedented opportunities to streamline workflows and enhance viewer experiences. Staying abreast of the latest innovations will empower creators to leverage AI-driven automation to its fullest potential, promising long-term success on YouTube.

In conclusion, the journey through the dynamic world of automated account management has unveiled the transformative potential of AI technologies in optimizing workflows, engaging with audiences, and driving channel growth. The future beckons with promises of advancements that will further streamline processes, offering creators a canvas where creativity meets efficiency, a space where content is not just created but celebrated. By embracing the potent synergy of AI and automated account management, creators stand on the cusp of a revolution, ready to carve out a niche in the vibrant YouTube landscape, fostering a space of innovation, engagement, and unprecedented growth. Let us forge ahead in this journey of content creation, with AI as our ally, ready to embrace a future brimming with possibilities and success in the exhilarating space of YouTube.

Chapter 8
AI for Data Analytics and Insights

In today's data-centric environment, organizations increasingly rely on AI-powered data analytics to garner invaluable insights and guide informed decisions. This chapter unfolds the fundamental concepts and methodologies central to AI-powered data analytics, a critical tool in steering business triumphs. By harnessing the capabilities of AI algorithms and techniques, entities can unlock the hidden potential of their data, unveiling insights that act as catalysts in optimizing operations, enhancing customer experiences, and fostering growth.

AI algorithms stand as pivotal forces in data collection and analysis, empowering organizations to sift through and understand vast amounts of data with precision and efficiency. These algorithms function as vigilant sentinels, identifying patterns, trends, and correlations within data, fostering actionable insights that fuel strategic decision-making.

Venturing further, we find the vibrant world of data visualization, a potent tool in articulating complex data through visually captivating narratives. AI-driven techniques enhance this process, automating the generation of interactive and visually arresting visualizations, facilitating a seamless interpretation and analysis of data for stakeholders. The deployment of AI-powered data visualization tools translates to effective communication of insights, patterns, and trends, steering organizations towards data-driven decision-making.

Predictive analytics beckons with a promise of proactive decision-making, leveraging historical data and AI algorithms to forecast future occurrences. This foresight allows entities to identify potential risks and opportunities, optimizing business strategies with a vision grounded in data.

In the vast ocean of data, anomalies and outliers often hold the key to valuable insights, signaling potential issues or opportunities. AI algorithms, equipped with techniques like clustering and supervised learning, excel in detecting deviations from the norm, aiding organizations in identifying fraud, errors, or emerging trends. This proactive approach to anomaly detection enhances operational efficiency, mitigates risks, and fosters data-driven decisions, steering organizations towards a path of growth and stability.

In the dynamic sphere of social media, a treasure trove of data awaits, offering insights into customer behavior, preferences, and trends. AI-powered tools stand as diligent miners in this environment, analyzing social media content, sentiment, and engagement metrics to offer actionable insights on a range of topics including customer sentiment, brand perception, and campaign performance. Leveraging these tools enables organizations to fine-tune their social media strategies, enhancing customer engagement and fostering a positive brand image.

As we forge ahead, we encounter sentiment analysis and opinion mining, techniques that delve into text data to extract customer sentiment and opinions. AI algorithms stand as powerful tools in this domain, analyzing text data from diverse sources such as customer reviews, social media posts, and surveys to gauge sentiment, emotions, and opinions. This deep understanding of customer preferences facilitates improved satisfaction and fosters data-driven decisions, steering organizations towards a path of success and growth.

Understanding the intricacies of diverse customer groups through segmentation and profiling emerges as a cornerstone in crafting tailored marketing strategies. AI algorithms stand as powerful tools in this endeavor, meticulously analyzing customer data to carve out distinct segments grounded in demographic, behavioral, and psychographic characteristics. Techniques such as clustering and classification come to the fore, processing vast datasets to segment customers with pinpoint accuracy. By embracing AI-driven customer segmentation and profiling, organizations find themselves equipped to personalize marketing initiatives, hone customer targeting strategies, and elevate the overall customer experience to unprecedented heights.

As we venture further, we find ourselves in the realm of real-time data analytics, a domain that empowers organizations to analyze and respond to data as it streams in, offering actionable insights on a real-time basis. AI algorithms showcase their prowess in processing this streaming data, delivering timely insights that facilitate data-driven decisions in real-time. This dynamic approach to data analytics enhances operational efficiency, allowing organizations to identify emerging trends and issues swiftly, and adapt to the fluctuating market dynamics with agility and foresight.

Looking towards the horizon, we see the field of AI in a state of relentless evolution, with its imprint on data analytics and insights poised to expand exponentially. Groundbreaking advancements such as augmented analytics, automated machine learning, and natural language processing hold the promise to redefine the contours of data analytics, unveiling new avenues of possibilities for organizations globally. By keeping a finger on the pulse of the latest AI trends and harnessing the transformative power of AI in data analytics, organizations can carve out a competitive edge, fostering a culture of innovation that stands as a harbinger of success in their respective industries.

As we draw this chapter to a close, we reflect on the pivotal role of AI-powered data analytics and insights in the contemporary data-driven world. Organizations aspiring to flourish in this dynamic landscape find a powerful ally in AI, a technology that offers the tools and techniques to mine valuable insights from data, optimizing operations and enhancing customer experiences to foster growth. The road ahead for AI in data analytics is laden with immense potential, a journey of evolution that promises to redefine the paradigms of business success.

In conclusion, we stand at a juncture where the fusion of AI algorithms and techniques with data analytics emerges as a beacon of potential, guiding organizations to extract the utmost value from their data reservoirs. This synergy promises to optimize operations, refine customer experiences, and foster growth, steering organizations towards a trajectory of success in a landscape that is ever-evolving.

As we envisage the future, it is replete with opportunities, a future where AI-driven data analytics holds the key to unlocking unprecedented avenues of innovation and success. Organizations that embrace this potent synergy will find themselves well-positioned to navigate the complex and dynamic landscape of business success, steering towards a future where data is not just a resource but a catalyst for innovation, growth, and sustained success in the competitive market space. Let us embrace this vibrant future, leveraging the transformative potential of AI in data analytics, as we forge ahead in a world brimming with opportunities, guided by insights and driven by data.

Chapter 9
AI for Community Management

In the bustling ecosystem of YouTube, community management stands as a linchpin in fostering a loyal and engaged audience. Content creators find themselves in a space where active engagement and interaction with viewers are not just beneficial but essential. Recognizing the gravity of community management allows creators to carve out a niche where positivity and engagement thrive, a space where every viewer feels seen and valued.

AI technologies come to the fore in this endeavor, offering tools that can streamline community management, making it a less daunting task. These technologies facilitate a nurturing environment where creators can foster a positive and thriving community on their YouTube channels. By leveraging AI, creators can ensure that their community management strategies are not just efficient but also effective, fostering a space where viewers come for the content and stay for the community.

As YouTube channels burgeon, managing comments becomes a Herculean task, one fraught with challenges that can sometimes be overwhelming for content creators. AI algorithms stand as powerful allies in this endeavor, offering automation solutions for comment moderation, spam detection, and engagement. These AI-powered tools sift through comments, filtering out offensive or inappropriate content, thereby safeguarding the sanctity of the community space.

This filtration process ensures that creators can focus their energies on engaging with genuine viewers, fostering a positive community environment where healthy discussions and interactions are encouraged. By automating the moderation process, creators can maintain a space that is respectful and inclusive, a space where every viewer feels safe to express their opinions and share their thoughts.

In the dynamic YouTube environment, keeping viewers engaged is a task that requires not just great content but also a deep understanding of viewer preferences and interests. AI-driven recommendation systems offer a solution, suggesting videos, playlists, and other content that aligns seamlessly with the interests of the viewers. These personalized recommendations foster a sense of community, encouraging viewers to actively engage with the content, thereby creating a loyal viewer base that returns time and again.

Sentiment analysis, a technique that leverages AI algorithms, offers insights into viewer emotions and reactions, providing a nuanced understanding of viewer feedback and preferences. These tools analyze a plethora of indicators including comment sentiment, likes, and dislikes, painting a comprehensive picture of viewer satisfaction. Armed with this data, content creators can make informed decisions, tweaking their content strategies to foster improved community engagement, creating content that resonates with their audience on a deeper level.

As we navigate further, we find that AI analytics hold the key to automating community insights, offering a deep dive into community engagement, demographics, and content performance. These tools automate the process of data collection, reporting, and insights generation, offering a treasure trove of information that can guide content creators in refining their community management strategies.

By analyzing viewer behavior, creators can gain a deeper understanding of their audience, allowing them to tailor their content to better meet viewer preferences. This personalized approach ensures that viewers find content that resonates with them, fostering a community where engagement is not just encouraged but celebrated.

In the ever-evolving YouTube space, the role of community management is pivotal, and the task of actively engaging with viewers and addressing their feedback and queries is of utmost importance. Here, AI-powered chatbots and voice assistants come into play, offering a helping hand to content creators in managing user interactions with efficiency and responsiveness. These AI-driven tools have the capability to automatically respond to common viewer queries, guiding them to relevant content and providing necessary information, thereby enhancing the community engagement manifold.

Moreover, these tools foster a responsive communication channel, where viewers feel heard and valued, creating a space where interaction is not just a feature but a fundamental pillar of community building. Leveraging AI in this facet ensures a seamless and enriched viewer experience, fostering a community where every interaction adds value and builds a stronger bond between the creator and the viewers.

As we steer towards building a supportive and inclusive community, the proactive role of content creators becomes evident. AI tools and techniques stand as powerful allies in this endeavor, offering insights into user behavior, language patterns, and engagement metrics. These insights allow creators to identify potential community members who resonate with the channel's values, nurturing a space where like-minded individuals come together in a harmonious blend of ideas and discussions.

Furthermore, sentiment analysis and AI-driven user feedback tools offer a goldmine of information for content refinement. These tools provide a nuanced understanding of viewer preferences, helping creators to tailor their content strategies to better align with viewer expectations. By addressing viewer concerns and incorporating feedback, creators foster a space where content evolution is a collaborative process, a journey undertaken together with the community.

In any community, conflicts are inevitable, and the YouTube space is no exception. AI technologies offer solutions here too, facilitating conflict resolution and fostering community harmony. These technologies have the prowess to detect and analyze contentious conversations, offering insights and strategies for de-escalation and mediation. This proactive approach ensures a supportive and inclusive community environment, where conflicts are resolved with empathy and understanding, fostering a space of harmony and mutual respect.

As we envision the future of community management, we see a landscape rich with opportunities, a space where AI technologies are not just tools but essential companions in the journey of community building. The emerging trends and innovations in AI-driven community management tools promise a future where insights and recommendations are more accurate and tailored to the unique dynamics of each community.

By keeping abreast of the latest developments in AI, creators can harness the transformative potential of these technologies, fostering communities that are not just engaged but thriving, a space where every viewer finds a sense of belonging and every content creator finds a loyal and engaged audience.

In conclusion, the journey of community management is one of continuous evolution, a path where AI technologies stand as powerful allies, offering tools and insights that foster engagement, inclusivity, and harmony. As we forge ahead in the dynamic YouTube space, let us embrace the transformative potential of AI in community management, creating spaces that are vibrant, inclusive, and engaged, fostering communities that resonate with positivity and mutual respect. Let us envision a future where AI empowers creators to build communities that are not just audiences but families, a space where every viewer is a valued member, and every interaction is a step towards building a stronger, more engaged, and harmonious community.

In the rapidly changing world of YouTube, community management emerges as a cornerstone, vital in nurturing a loyal and engaged audience. Content creators are tasked with the essential role of fostering active engagement and interaction with viewers, a role that goes beyond merely producing content. Recognizing the pivotal role of community management, creators are encouraged to foster environments where positivity and engagement are not just buzzwords but the very essence of their YouTube channels.

AI technologies stand as formidable allies in this endeavor, offering a suite of tools that streamline the community management process, transforming it from a daunting task to a manageable and even enjoyable part of content creation. These tools facilitate a nurturing environment, where creators can foster a positive and thriving community on their YouTube channels, a space where viewers are not just spectators but active participants in a vibrant community.

As YouTube channels grow, the task of managing comments becomes increasingly complex, necessitating a robust system to moderate comments and maintain a healthy discussion environment. Here, AI algorithms prove to be invaluable, offering solutions that automate comment moderation and spam detection, thereby preserving the sanctity of the community space. This automation allows creators to focus on genuine engagement, fostering a community where respect and inclusivity are the norm.

To keep viewers engaged, creators must go beyond producing great content; they must understand and cater to viewer preferences and interests. AI-driven recommendation systems are instrumental in this, suggesting videos, playlists, and other content that aligns with viewers' interests, fostering a sense of community and encouraging active engagement. This personalized approach to content recommendation ensures a loyal viewer base that returns time and again, drawn in by a creator who understands and values their preferences.

Sentiment analysis, powered by AI algorithms, offers a nuanced understanding of viewer feedback, providing insights into viewer emotions and reactions. These tools analyze various indicators, including comment sentiment and likes/dislikes, offering a comprehensive understanding of viewer satisfaction. Armed with this data, creators can fine-tune their content strategies, fostering improved community engagement and creating content that resonates deeply with their audience.

Looking ahead, we see a future rich with opportunities, a future where AI technologies are integral in the journey of community building. The emerging trends and innovations in AI-driven community management tools hold the promise of a more personalized and engaged community experience, offering insights and recommendations that are finely tuned to the unique dynamics of each community.

By staying informed about the latest developments in AI, creators can leverage the transformative potential of these technologies, fostering communities that are not just engaged but thriving, a space where every viewer finds a sense of belonging and every content creator finds a loyal and engaged audience.

In conclusion, community management on YouTube is a dynamic and multifaceted endeavor, one that stands central to building a loyal and engaged audience. As we forge ahead in this dynamic space, the role of AI technologies as powerful allies becomes increasingly apparent, offering tools and insights that foster engagement, inclusivity, and harmony. Let us embrace the transformative potential of AI in community management, creating spaces that are vibrant, inclusive, and engaged, fostering communities that resonate with positivity and mutual respect. Let us envision a future where AI empowers creators to build communities that are not just audiences but families, a space where every viewer is a valued member, and every interaction is a step towards building a stronger, more engaged, and harmonious community.

Chapter 10
Leveraging AI for Content Monetization

In the ever-competitive sphere of YouTube, content monetization stands as a pivotal mechanism that facilitates channel growth and sustainability. It is a process that goes beyond merely generating revenue, serving as a vital tool that supports creators both creatively and financially. Understanding the nuances of content monetization is not just beneficial but essential for creators aspiring to carve out a sustainable path in the YouTube ecosystem.

At this juncture, it is imperative to acknowledge the transformative role of AI technologies in enhancing the scope and effectiveness of content monetization strategies. By harnessing the capabilities of AI, creators can unlock avenues to maximize their revenue potential, thereby finding the financial support necessary to foster creativity and maintain a vibrant YouTube channel. The integration of AI technologies in monetization strategies promises not just enhanced revenue streams but also a pathway to achieving a harmonious balance between monetization and viewer satisfaction.

Turning our attention to the myriad ways AI can augment revenue opportunities, we find a landscape rich with potential. AI stands as a powerful ally, offering creators a suite of tools and strategies to optimize revenue streams effectively. One such strategy is dynamic ad placement, a technique that leverages AI algorithms to identify the optimal moments within a video to place ads, thereby ensuring a positive viewer experience while maximizing ad effectiveness.

In addition to dynamic ad placement, creators have at their disposal programmatic advertising, a strategy that automates the ad buying process, targeting users more precisely and at scale.

This approach, coupled with targeted audience segmentation, allows creators to deliver personalized ad content to different viewer segments, enhancing the relevance of ads and fostering a more engaged viewer base. By embracing these AI-driven strategies, creators can navigate the complex landscape of YouTube monetization with a guided and informed approach, optimizing revenue streams while preserving the integrity of the viewer experience.

Advertising stands as a cornerstone in the monetization strategies of many YouTube creators, serving as a primary revenue stream that fuels growth and sustainability. In this context, AI-driven advertising strategies emerge as vital tools in enhancing monetization potential, offering a pathway to optimized ad monetization and higher revenue generation.

AI-powered tools offer a deep understanding of viewer demographics, watch history, and interests, insights that are instrumental in crafting personalized and relevant ad strategies. These tools analyze a plethora of data points, offering a nuanced understanding of viewer preferences and behaviors, thereby facilitating the delivery of ads that resonate with viewers on a deeper level. This personalized approach to advertising not only enhances the viewer experience but also fosters higher engagement rates, translating to increased revenue potential for creators.

By leveraging AI-driven advertising strategies, creators can craft advertising narratives that are not just personalized but deeply resonant with their audience, fostering a space where ads are viewed not as interruptions but as complementary content that adds value to the viewer experience. This harmonious integration of content and advertising stands as a testament to the transformative potential of AI in content monetization, offering a pathway to sustainable and lucrative monetization strategies.

In conclusion, as we navigate the complex and dynamic world of YouTube content monetization, the role of AI technologies emerges as both transformative and pivotal. Creators find in AI a powerful ally, offering tools and insights that promise to redefine the paradigms of content monetization. As we forge ahead in this vibrant space, let us embrace the potential of AI technologies, leveraging their capabilities to craft monetization strategies that are not just effective but also harmonious, fostering a YouTube ecosystem where creativity thrives, and monetization serves as a catalyst for sustained growth and innovation. Let us envision a future where AI empowers creators to find financial success without compromising on the quality and integrity of their content, a future where monetization and creativity go hand in hand, guided by the transformative potential of AI in content monetization.

In the dynamic YouTube environment, the pursuit of optimal revenue streams is a continuous endeavor, and here, AI-based revenue optimization techniques emerge as potent tools in a creator's arsenal. These techniques, grounded in the analytical prowess of AI algorithms, offer a pathway to maximize earnings potential through a meticulous analysis of various factors including ad placement, bidding strategies, and revenue share models.

One such technique is dynamic pricing, a strategy that leverages AI to analyze viewer engagement and ad performance, thereby determining the optimal pricing strategy for ad placements. This approach, coupled with yield management, ensures that creators can optimize revenue generation, finding the sweet spot where viewer engagement meets revenue optimization. By embracing these AI-driven strategies, creators can navigate the complex waters of revenue optimization with a guided and informed approach, ensuring a monetization strategy that is both lucrative and viewer-friendly.

As we delve deeper, we find that data analytics stands as a cornerstone in the revenue analysis and optimization process. AI-powered data analytics tools offer creators a deep understanding of revenue data, extracting valuable insights that can guide revenue optimization strategies. These tools analyze a plethora of data points, including ad performance, audience segmentation, and revenue trends, painting a comprehensive picture of a channel's revenue landscape.

Armed with these insights, creators can craft revenue optimization strategies that are not just informed but also tailored to the unique dynamics of their audience. This personalized approach to revenue optimization ensures a strategy that is both effective and resonant with viewers, fostering a space where monetization goes hand in hand with viewer satisfaction. By harnessing the capabilities of AI in data analytics, creators find themselves equipped with the tools necessary to make informed decisions, maximizing revenue potential while preserving the integrity of the viewer experience.

As we forge ahead, we find that the YouTube space offers creators avenues to diversify their revenue streams through content merchandising and brand partnerships. AI algorithms serve as diligent assistants in this endeavor, analyzing viewer preferences, purchase behavior, and offering related product recommendations. This analysis facilitates content merchandising strategies that are not just effective but also deeply resonant with the audience, fostering a space where viewers find value not just in the content but also in the curated product recommendations.

Furthermore, AI-powered tools offer support in identifying and securing brand partnerships, a process that leverages insights into audience demographics, engagement metrics, and brand alignment. These tools offer a pathway to build long-term brand collaborations, partnerships that are grounded in mutual value and aligned visions. By embracing AI-driven strategies in content merchandising and brand partnerships, creators can foster a YouTube space that is not just creative but also financially sustainable, a space where revenue streams are diversified and opportunities for growth are abundant.

In the YouTube ecosystem, revenue fraud emerges as a significant impediment, posing substantial risks to content creators. AI comes to the rescue, offering robust solutions for detecting and preventing revenue fraud through vigilant automated monitoring and analysis. These AI algorithms are adept at identifying fraudulent activities, including click fraud and ad viewability manipulation, employing anomaly detection and pattern recognition techniques to safeguard creators' revenue streams.

By leveraging AI-driven fraud detection and prevention strategies, creators can foster a platform that stands on the pillars of fairness and transparency. This proactive approach ensures that creators can focus on crafting quality content without the looming threat of revenue fraud, fostering a space where creativity flourishes, and revenue streams remain secure and unhampered.

As we transition into the realm of content licensing and distribution, we find that AI algorithms play a pivotal role in unlocking additional revenue opportunities for YouTube creators. These technologies facilitate content licensing through meticulous analysis of copyright ownership and the management of licensing agreements. Moreover, AI-powered tools aid creators in fine-tuning their content distribution strategies, identifying target markets, localizing content, and recommending the most effective distribution channels.

By embracing AI-driven strategies for content licensing and distribution, creators can amplify their global reach and revenue potential. This approach ensures a broader audience base, reaching viewers across different geographies and demographics, thereby creating a content ecosystem that is both diverse and inclusive. Through AI's guidance, creators can navigate the complex pathways of content distribution with a strategy that is both informed and targeted, ensuring content reaches the right audience at the right time, maximizing both viewer engagement and revenue potential.

As we venture further, we encounter audience-supported monetization models, avenues that offer creators alternative revenue streams through crowdfunding and subscription services. AI stands as a guiding force in this endeavor, analyzing viewer engagement, preferences, and their willingness to support creators financially. These AI-powered tools facilitate the creation and management of crowdfunding campaigns, subscription-based content, and Patreon-like models, providing recommendations for pricing, membership tiers, and rewards based on a deep understanding of the audience's preferences and behaviors.

Leveraging AI in this facet of monetization fosters a community of strong and loyal supporters, a community where viewers are not just spectators but active participants in a creator's journey. This collaborative approach to monetization ensures a symbiotic relationship between creators and viewers, fostering a YouTube space that thrives on mutual support and shared success.

Looking ahead, we find ourselves on the cusp of a revolution in content monetization, a future rich with opportunities fostered by advancements in AI technologies. Emerging trends such as blockchain-based monetization, AI-driven revenue sharing models, and microtransactions beckon, offering creators innovative avenues to monetize their content. These advancements promise to reshape the contours of content monetization, introducing models that are both innovative and aligned with the evolving dynamics of the YouTube platform.

By staying informed about the latest innovations in AI and its integration with emerging technologies, creators can stay ahead of the curve, exploring new pathways for content monetization that are both lucrative and sustainable. This forward-thinking approach ensures a future where content monetization is not just a revenue-generating mechanism but a collaborative and innovative space, fostering a YouTube ecosystem that thrives on creativity, innovation, and mutual growth.

In conclusion, as we reflect on the transformative potential of AI in content monetization, we find ourselves envisioning a YouTube space that is both vibrant and sustainable. A space where creators are empowered with the tools and insights to craft monetization strategies that are not just effective but also harmonious with the viewer experience. A space where monetization serves as a catalyst for sustained growth and innovation, fostering a symbiotic relationship between creators and viewers.

As we forge ahead, let us embrace the transformative potential of AI in content monetization, steering towards a future where creativity and monetization go hand in hand, guided by the innovative prowess of AI technologies. Let us envision a future where AI empowers creators to find financial success without compromising on the quality and integrity of their content, a future where monetization and creativity thrive in harmony, fostering a YouTube ecosystem that is both lucrative and vibrant, a space where every creator finds the tools to succeed, and every viewer finds content that is both enriching and valuable. Let us steer towards this vibrant future, leveraging the transformative potential of AI in content monetization, forging a path that is guided by innovation, driven by data, and grounded in the collaborative spirit of the YouTube community.

Chapter 11
AI and Accessibility on YouTube

In the digital age, the emphasis on accessibility in online platforms is ever-increasing, paving the way for a more inclusive and universal user experience. YouTube, being a frontrunner in the content creation space, stands at the forefront of this transformation, with artificial intelligence (AI) serving as a pivotal tool in enhancing accessibility features, thereby broadening the spectrum of audience engagement.

A cornerstone in this endeavor is the integration of closed captions, a feature that has revolutionized content accessibility on YouTube. Delving into the role of AI in automatic caption generation, we find that it serves as a vital tool in making content accessible to a diverse audience, including individuals with hearing impairments. AI facilitates this through the utilization of speech recognition technology, a mechanism that transcribes audio into text, thereby creating a textual representation of the auditory content.

AI algorithms are central to this process, enabling the generation of closed captions that are both accurate and timely. This precision ensures that videos become more accessible and engaging, catering to a wide array of audiences with varying needs and preferences. By fostering an environment where content is universally accessible, creators can ensure that their message reaches a wider audience, fostering a space of inclusivity and understanding.

As we further dissect the benefits of accurate and timely closed captions, we find that they cater to a diverse viewership, extending beyond individuals with hearing impairments to include non-native speakers and individuals in noisy environments. Moreover, they serve as a valuable tool for individuals with cognitive disabilities, enhancing comprehension and fostering a more inclusive viewing experience. AI-powered closed captions stand as a beacon of inclusivity, enhancing engagement and comprehension for a diverse viewer base. This inclusivity ensures that content resonates with a broader audience, fostering a YouTube space that is both diverse and universal, where every viewer finds content that is accessible, engaging, and enriching.

However, the journey towards perfecting AI-generated closed captions is ongoing, with ample room for enhancement. Strategies to improve the quality of these captions are manifold, including the refinement of speech recognition algorithms to reduce errors and foster accuracy. Moreover, providing options for manual editing ensures that creators can fine-tune captions, ensuring a level of precision that is tailored to their content.

By focusing on enhancing the quality of AI-generated captions, creators can foster a space where captions are not just an accessory but a vital tool in content accessibility. This focus on quality ensures that captions are reliable, fostering a viewer experience that is both enriching and inclusive.

As we envision the future of AI and accessibility on YouTube, we find ourselves amidst a transformative phase, where AI stands as a powerful ally in fostering accessibility. The integration of AI in enhancing closed captions is just the tip of the iceberg, with immense potential for further advancements in this space.

Looking ahead, we see a YouTube platform that is universally accessible, a space where every individual, regardless of their physical abilities or linguistic proficiency, can engage with content in a meaningful way. AI serves as a catalyst in this transformation, offering tools and technologies that promise to redefine the paradigms of accessibility on YouTube.

The role of artificial intelligence (AI) in enhancing accessibility continues to be a focal point, with translations and multilingual support emerging as significant areas where AI can foster inclusivity and broaden audience reach.

A remarkable stride in this direction is the facilitation of real-time translation for global audiences, a feature that stands to revolutionize multilingual support on YouTube. AI algorithms are at the helm of this transformation, translating speech seamlessly into various languages, thereby unlocking content for users worldwide. This real-time translation ensures that viewers can access and comprehend content in their preferred language, fostering a space where language is no longer a barrier but a bridge to a richer, more inclusive content experience.

While automated translations have indeed come a long way, courtesy of advancements in AI, the journey towards achieving flawless accuracy and fluency is ongoing. Techniques such as neural machine translation and context-aware algorithms are being harnessed to enhance the quality of translations, aiming to bridge language barriers effectively for global audiences. By focusing on improving the accuracy and fluency of translations, AI stands as a powerful tool in fostering a YouTube space that is truly global, where content transcends linguistic barriers to reach a diverse and expansive audience.

Furthermore, multilingual support serves as a catalyst in expanding reach and engagement, offering content creators a pathway to attract international audiences. This AI-powered support not only increases viewership but fosters a sense of inclusivity, creating a space where every viewer finds content that resonates with them, irrespective of the language they speak.

As we transition into the realm of audio description, we find that AI holds the potential to redefine accessibility for visually impaired viewers. Leveraging computer vision technology, AI can describe visual elements within videos, offering visually impaired individuals a comprehensive understanding of the visual content. This transformative approach ensures that visually impaired viewers can fully appreciate the visual narrative, fostering a richer and more inclusive viewing experience.

However, the journey towards perfecting AI-generated audio descriptions is a continuous one, with a focus on enhancing the quality and detail of these descriptions. Techniques such as advanced object recognition and scene analysis algorithms are being employed to improve audio descriptions, aiming to offer visually impaired viewers a more immersive and engaging experience. This focus on detail ensures a nuanced understanding of visual content, fostering an experience that is both enriching and inclusive.

Moreover, audio description stands as a tool that enhances not only inclusivity but the overall viewer experience. It fosters empathy, enriches storytelling, and creates a more inclusive online community, serving as a bridge that connects viewers to content on a deeper, more empathetic level. By focusing on the positive impact of audio description, creators can foster a YouTube community that is not only inclusive but empathetic, a space where every viewer finds content that is accessible, engaging, and enriching.

As we envision the future of AI and accessibility on YouTube, we find ourselves amidst a transformative phase, where AI stands as a powerful ally in fostering accessibility. The integration of AI in enhancing closed captions is just the tip of the iceberg, with immense potential for further advancements in this space.

Looking ahead, we see a YouTube platform that is universally accessible, a space where every individual, regardless of their physical abilities or linguistic proficiency, can engage with content in a meaningful way. AI serves as a catalyst in this transformation, offering tools and technologies that promise to redefine the paradigms of accessibility on YouTube.

AI's role in enhancing accessibility continues to evolve, with visual recognition and object identification emerging as pivotal areas where AI can foster inclusivity and enhance the user experience for individuals with visual impairments.

AI-powered visual recognition technology stands as a beacon of empowerment for individuals with visual impairments, offering them a pathway to understand and interact with visual content in a meaningful way. Through the analysis and description of images and videos, AI algorithms facilitate a deeper engagement with content, ensuring that visually impaired users can immerse themselves in the visual narrative, transcending barriers and fostering inclusivity.

Furthermore, AI facilitates a more accessible interaction with videos, identifying key elements within the content and offering audio cues to guide visually impaired viewers. This approach ensures a full engagement with the content, creating a space where visual impairments are not a barrier to enjoying the rich tapestry of visual narratives available on YouTube.

As we delve deeper, we find that the accuracy of object identification is a cornerstone in enhancing accessibility, with advancements in AI algorithms, such as deep learning and convolutional neural networks, playing a pivotal role. These advancements foster a seamless experience, where visually impaired viewers can navigate content with ease, marking a significant stride towards a more inclusive YouTube space.

Transitioning into the realm of user interface customization, we find that AI stands as a powerful tool in personalizing the YouTube interface to cater to individual needs. Through adaptive design and customization options, AI facilitates a tailored viewing experience, where elements such as font size, color contrast, and navigation preferences are adapted to suit individual requirements, fostering a YouTube space that is both inclusive and accessible.

Moreover, AI empowers users to take control of their viewing experiences, offering them the tools to create personalized and accessible interfaces. This user-driven approach ensures that every individual can craft a viewing experience that suits their unique needs, fostering a space where accessibility is not just offered but personalized to cater to individual preferences.

As we navigate further, we find ourselves in the realm of AI-powered recommendations, a space where AI algorithms play a crucial role in fostering diversity and inclusivity. By considering accessibility preferences in video recommendations, AI fosters a content ecosystem that is both diverse and representative, creating a YouTube space that celebrates diversity in all its forms.

Furthermore, AI offers the potential to tailor recommendations based on individual accessibility preferences, learning and adapting to users' choices to offer recommendations that align with their unique needs. This personalized approach ensures that every user finds content that resonates with them, fostering a YouTube space that is both inclusive and personalized.

However, the journey towards AI-powered recommendations is not without its challenges, with ethical concerns and biases emerging as significant hurdles. Strategies such as enhancing transparency in recommendation algorithms and fostering diversity in training data are being explored to address these concerns, ensuring that AI-powered recommendations are fair, unbiased, and inclusive.

As we envision the future of AI and accessibility on YouTube, we find ourselves amidst a transformative journey, where AI stands as a powerful ally in fostering inclusivity and enhancing the user experience. Through advancements in visual recognition, user interface customization, and AI-powered recommendations, AI promises to redefine the paradigms of accessibility on YouTube, steering towards a future where every user finds a space of engagement that is both inclusive and enriching.

In conclusion, as we reflect on the transformative potential of AI in fostering accessibility on YouTube, we find ourselves envisioning a space that is both inclusive and universal. A space where AI technologies serve as enablers, fostering a platform where content is accessible to all, transcending barriers of language, disability, and environment.

As we forge ahead, let us embrace the transformative potential of AI in enhancing accessibility on YouTube, steering towards a future where content is not just viewed but experienced in its fullest form, a future where every viewer finds a space of engagement that is both inclusive and enriching. Let us steer towards this vibrant future, leveraging the transformative potential of AI in enhancing accessibility on YouTube, forging a path that is guided by innovation, driven by inclusivity, and grounded in the universal language of understanding and empathy.

Collaborations for accessibility emerge as a vital frontier where partnerships between YouTube and various accessibility organizations play a pivotal role. These collaborations, grounded in a shared vision of inclusivity, have fostered advancements in accessibility features, bringing together advocacy groups, accessibility experts, and developers in a collective endeavor to enhance the YouTube experience for all.

We will delve into the heart of these collaborations, highlighting successful initiatives and case studies that have brought remarkable improvements in accessibility on YouTube. These narratives of success not only serve as testament to the transformative power of collaborative efforts but also as a beacon of inspiration, encouraging future collaborations grounded in innovation and a shared commitment to inclusivity.

As we gaze into the future, we envisage a vibrant landscape of collaborative efforts, where YouTube, content creators, AI experts, and accessibility organizations come together in a symphony of cross-disciplinary collaborations. Through the lens of AI, these collaborations hold the promise of fostering a more inclusive online video community, a space where accessibility is not just a feature but a fundamental pillar of the YouTube experience.

Turning our attention to the impact on content creators, we find that AI-powered accessibility features stand as powerful allies, enhancing discoverability and fostering a deeper connection with a diverse audience. These features not only enhance the viewing experience but also inspire creators to explore new horizons of content that prioritize inclusivity.
However, the journey towards AI-driven accessibility is not without its hurdles, with creators harboring concerns about the integration of these features. Addressing these concerns head-on, we aim to provide insights that alleviate fears and encourage creators to embrace the transformative potential of AI in enhancing accessibility, fostering a space where creativity and inclusivity walk hand in hand.

As we navigate the complex terrain of ethical considerations and challenges, we find ourselves amidst a discourse where privacy and data protection emerge as vital concerns. The reliance on user data necessitates a thoughtful approach to privacy, with strategies such as anonymization and transparency taking center stage in ensuring ethical and responsible data handling.

Furthermore, the journey towards AI-driven accessibility brings us face to face with the challenge of biases in AI algorithms. Through a careful and continuous evaluation, we aim to mitigate these biases, fostering a space where AI-driven accessibility features are grounded in fairness and inclusivity.

As we forge ahead, we find ourselves balancing on the delicate line between automation and human involvement, a balance that is pivotal in addressing the nuances of accessibility. Through a harmonious blend of AI and human insight, we aim to foster a YouTube space that is both scalable and nuanced, a space where technology and humanity come together in a dance of harmony.

In the final leg of our journey, we find ourselves amidst a tapestry of case studies and success stories, narratives that highlight the successful implementation of AI-powered accessibility features on YouTube. These narratives, rich with lessons and insights, offer a roadmap for content creators and YouTube alike, guiding them towards a future where accessibility is not just a feature but a cornerstone of the YouTube experience.

As we draw this chapter to a close, we find ourselves reflecting on the transformative journey of AI in enhancing accessibility on YouTube. Through the lens of AI, we have traversed a landscape rich with innovations, from closed captions and translations to visual recognition and user interface customization.

Looking towards the future, we envision a YouTube space that continues to evolve, a space where AI-driven accessibility shapes the contours of inclusivity, fostering a platform where every viewer finds a space of engagement that is both inclusive and enriching.

In conclusion, we stand on the threshold of a vibrant future, a future where AI-driven accessibility continues to redefine the paradigms of inclusivity on YouTube. As we forge ahead, let us embrace the transformative potential of AI, steering towards a future where YouTube is not just a platform for content but a space of universal accessibility, a space where every viewer, irrespective of their abilities, finds a home of engagement, understanding, and inclusivity. Let us steer towards this vibrant future, with AI as our ally, forging a path that is guided by innovation, driven by inclusivity, and grounded in the universal language of understanding and empathy.

Chapter 12
Machine Learning for YouTube Creators

The rise of machine learning has had a profound impact on various industries, and YouTube is no exception. In this chapter, we will explore the ways in which machine learning algorithms can assist creators in enhancing their videos. From automated video editing to audience engagement and personalized recommendations, the possibilities are endless. Let's dive into the world of machine learning for YouTube creators and uncover its potential.

The process of video editing is time-consuming and requires technical skills. However, with the advent of machine learning, creators can now leverage AI-powered tools for automatic video editing. These algorithms analyze the content, identify key moments, and generate a professionally edited video. The benefits of automated video editing are significant, as it saves valuable time and effort for creators. However, it's important to acknowledge the limitations of AI-powered tools. While they excel at basic editing tasks, they might lack the creative intuition and personal touch that human editors bring. Therefore, it is crucial for creators to customize and fine-tune the automated editing process to match their unique preferences and style.

Understanding audience preferences and staying on top of trends is crucial for YouTube creators. Machine learning algorithms can help in analyzing video content and identifying trends. By analyzing large volumes of data, AI can provide insights into what types of content are resonating with the audience, allowing creators to tailor their content strategy accordingly. Furthermore, AI algorithms enable creators to predict future trends and adapt their content strategies in anticipation of upcoming shifts in the YouTube landscape. This empowers creators to stay relevant and engage with their audience more effectively.

Audience engagement is vital for the success of YouTube creators, and machine learning algorithms can greatly enhance this aspect. By analyzing viewer behavior and preferences, AI-powered predictive analytics can provide creators with valuable insights. These insights help creators understand what content resonates with their audience and enable them to create more engaging and relevant videos. With the help of AI, creators can personalize their content recommendations, optimize video length, and improve overall viewer experience. By leveraging AI insights, creators can foster stronger connections with their audience and ultimately increase their reach and engagement.

Optimizing video metadata is crucial for maximizing discoverability and reach on YouTube. Machine learning algorithms offer AI-powered tools for optimizing video titles, descriptions, and tags. These tools analyze keywords, search trends, and viewer behavior to suggest relevant and SEO-friendly metadata. By leveraging these AI-driven optimization strategies, creators can improve the visibility of their videos and increase their chances of reaching a wider audience. It's important for creators to stay up-to-date with the latest advancements in AI-driven SEO techniques to stay ahead in the competitive world of YouTube.

Timely feedback and understanding key performance metrics are essential for optimizing content strategy. AI algorithms can provide real-time feedback on video performance, allowing creators to make data-driven decisions. By measuring key performance metrics such as watch time, engagement, and viewer retention, machine learning algorithms provide valuable insights into the effectiveness of a creator's content. Through AI-driven analytics, creators can identify areas for improvement, refine their content strategy, and ultimately achieve better results on YouTube.

Collaboration is an integral part of content creation, and machine learning can significantly enhance this process. By harnessing the power of AI, creators can leverage collaborative tools and platforms for seamless content creation and management. AI-powered tools enable real-time collaboration, automating tasks such as file sharing, version control, and feedback collection. This not only enhances productivity but also encourages creativity and innovation within teams. Machine learning algorithms can assist creators in finding potential collaborators based on their content preferences and past collaborations. By embracing collaborative AI platforms, creators can unlock the full potential of teamwork and create exceptional content together.

Understanding the unique preferences and characteristics of an audience is crucial for effective content creation. Machine learning algorithms excel at audience segmentation and targeting. By analyzing viewer data, AI algorithms can categorize audiences based on their interests, demographics, and behavior. This enables creators to customize content recommendations based on individual preferences, delivering a personalized viewing experience. By crafting personalized viewer experiences, creators can enhance engagement and build stronger connections with their audience, fostering loyalty and long-term viewership.

Accessibility is an important aspect of video content, and machine learning algorithms offer powerful tools for video transcription and translation. AI-powered video transcription technology can automatically generate accurate captions for videos, making them accessible to a wider audience, including those with hearing impairments or language barriers. Additionally, machine learning techniques ensure efficient and accurate video translation, allowing creators to expand their global reach. By leveraging AI-driven transcription and translation, creators can make their videos more inclusive, accessible, and appealing to diverse audiences.

Staying ahead of the ever-evolving YouTube algorithms is crucial for creators to maintain visibility and reach on the platform. Machine learning can assist creators in navigating algorithm updates and optimizing their content accordingly. By analyzing algorithm changes and understanding their impact on video rankings, AI algorithms provide insights into effective optimization techniques. Creators can leverage AI insights to refine their content, adapt their strategies, and maintain a competitive edge. By continually adapting to algorithm changes, creators can ensure their content remains relevant and continues to resonate with their target audience.

Monetization is a primary goal for many YouTube creators, and machine learning algorithms offer innovative strategies to maximize revenue. By identifying advertising opportunities and analyzing market trends, AI-powered algorithms can assist creators in optimizing their monetization strategies. AI-driven insights enable creators to make data-driven decisions when it comes to ad placements, sponsorships, and revenue generation. Furthermore, by understanding viewer behavior, AI algorithms can suggest effective monetization strategies tailored to their audience. The future of AI-driven monetization on YouTube holds great potential, and creators who leverage these strategies will be well-equipped to overcome potential challenges and thrive in the competitive landscape.

Throughout this chapter, we have explored the various ways machine learning can empower YouTube creators. From automated video editing and content analysis to audience engagement and personalized recommendations, machine learning algorithms offer a range of tools and insights to enhance the content creation process. By leveraging AI-driven strategies, creators can optimize their videos, engage with their audience more effectively, and stay ahead in the competitive landscape of YouTube. As machine learning continues to advance, the future holds even more possibilities for creators to leverage AI and create unbeatable content on YouTube.

Chapter 13
Deep Learning in Video Analysis

The field of deep learning has revolutionized various industries, and in the context of video analysis, it holds immense potential for extracting insights and patterns from videos. In this chapter, we will explore the concept of deep learning in video analysis and delve into its applications in object detection and recognition, scene understanding and segmentation, action recognition and activity understanding, emotion and sentiment analysis, speech and voice recognition, semantic annotation and metadata extraction, video-based recommendations and personalization, deep fake detection and authentication, as well as the challenges and ethical implications associated with deep learning in video analysis.

Looking into the field of video analysis, deep learning stands as a pillar, offering a rich set of tools and techniques that have transformed the way we analyze and interpret video content. Leveraging the power of convolutional neural networks (CNNs) and recurrent neural networks (RNNs), deep learning facilitates a range of applications, from object detection and recognition to scene understanding and action recognition, each of which we will discuss in detail in this chapter.

Starting with object detection and recognition, deep learning algorithms have proven to be a powerhouse, enabling accurate and efficient identification of objects in videos. These algorithms are trained on extensive datasets, learning to recognize objects in a variety of angles, sizes, lighting conditions, and backgrounds. This robust training ensures a high level of performance across different video contexts, from surveillance systems detecting suspicious objects to autonomous vehicles perceiving and reacting to their surroundings. The real-time analysis empowered by deep learning is indeed a game-changer in the field of video analysis.

Transitioning into scene understanding and segmentation, we find that deep learning techniques have significantly enhanced our ability to analyze visual cues and context in videos. CNNs stand at the forefront, extracting high-level features from video frames and inferring the overall scene to identify different elements within it. This process is further refined through semantic segmentation, where each pixel is labeled with its corresponding object or class, facilitating a detailed analysis and more accurate video interpretation. Applications such as video surveillance, video summarization, and augmented reality benefit immensely from deep scene understanding, offering a comprehensive insight into visual content.

Moving forward, we delve into the realm of action recognition and activity understanding, where deep learning plays a pivotal role. Utilizing recurrent neural networks (RNNs) and long short-term memory (LSTM) networks, these algorithms analyze motion patterns and temporal dependencies to accurately recognize actions in videos. The training process for these deep neural networks involves large-scale datasets, efficient architectures, and sophisticated training techniques, including transfer learning and reinforcement learning approaches. These methods enhance the performance of deep learning models, enabling them to recognize a wide range of human activities. Applications such as video surveillance, sports analytics, and human-computer interaction are revolutionized through deep learning-based action recognition, offering automated activity monitoring, behavioral analysis, and anomaly detection.

Reflecting on the advancements in deep learning for video analysis, we recognize the transformative potential it holds. From enhancing object recognition capabilities to facilitating deep scene understanding and accurate action recognition, deep learning stands as a powerful tool in the modern toolkit for video analysis. Its applications are vast, touching upon critical areas such as surveillance, autonomous vehicles, and augmented reality, to name a few.

Looking ahead, we envision a future where deep learning continues to evolve, offering even more sophisticated tools for video analysis. The integration of deep learning with other emerging technologies promises to unlock new potentials, fostering innovations that we can only begin to imagine. As we stand on the cusp of this exciting frontier, we anticipate a wave of developments that will further enhance our ability to analyze and interpret video content, opening up new avenues for innovation and discovery.

As we continue our journey through the intricate world of deep learning in video analysis, we find ourselves at the intersection of emotion and sentiment analysis. Here, deep learning algorithms stand as powerful tools, capable of dissecting facial expressions, vocal cues, and contextual information to gauge viewer reactions accurately. These algorithms, trained on extensive emotion-labeled datasets, can capture nuanced emotional cues, offering a rich understanding of complex emotions, individual differences, and context-dependent expressions. This understanding paves the way for content creators to craft videos that resonate deeply with viewers, fostering a heightened level of engagement and satisfaction.

Transitioning to the realm of speech and voice recognition, deep learning techniques have revolutionized the way we interpret auditory signals in videos. By harnessing large datasets of transcribed speech, recurrent neural networks (RNNs) and attention mechanisms work in harmony to capture temporal dependencies, enhancing the performance of speech recognition systems. These techniques, coupled with strategies such as data augmentation, multi-task learning, and domain adaptation, foster a robust and accurate speech recognition model, adaptable across various accents, languages, and environmental conditions. The applications are manifold, from improving video searchability to enhancing accessibility for individuals with hearing impairments, deep learning in speech recognition stands as a beacon of innovation.

Going further in, we encounter semantic annotation and metadata extraction, where deep learning algorithms work tirelessly to generate semantic annotations automatically. These algorithms analyze video frames, audio signals, and contextual data, extracting high-level features and inferring semantic meanings. The result is a rich tapestry of descriptive tags and metadata, enhancing video searchability and discoverability, and paving the way for a more accessible and relevant video content landscape.

As we navigate towards video-based recommendations and personalization, deep learning algorithms emerge as a potent force, analyzing viewing history, preferences, and contextual information to craft personalized video recommendations. These algorithms, grounded in recurrent neural networks (RNNs) and deep neural networks (DNNs), capture user behavior patterns, offering a more tailored viewing experience on YouTube. The integration of visual, textual, and behavioral data through multimodal deep learning algorithms fosters a holistic understanding of user preferences, enhancing user engagement and satisfaction.

As we approach the culmination of our discussion on deep learning in video analysis, we find ourselves confronted with the pressing issues of challenges and ethical implications. In the ever-evolving world of technology, the ethical compass must remain steadfast, guiding the development and deployment of deep learning models with fairness, transparency, and accountability at the forefront. This necessitates a vigilant approach to monitoring and minimizing biases in algorithms, fostering an environment where ethical concerns are not just addressed but actively mitigated.

A significant pillar in this ethical framework is the unwavering commitment to privacy and data protection. The onus is on the creators and technology providers to implement robust security measures, adhering to stringent privacy regulations that stand guard over user data. This ethical handling of data not only maintains user trust but also ensures the responsible stewardship of sensitive information, a cornerstone in the foundation of a reliable and secure digital space.

Navigating this complex terrain requires a harmonious collaboration and ongoing dialogue among technology providers, content creators, and users. A transparent discourse that seeks to constantly evaluate and address potential ethical implications, forging a path towards a more inclusive, fair, and responsible approach to video analysis. This collaborative endeavor, grounded in mutual respect and understanding, promises to usher in a new era of ethical deep learning applications in video analysis.

As we stand on the cusp of unprecedented advancements, we reflect on the transformative journey deep learning has embarked upon in the realm of video analysis on YouTube. From the intricate processes of object detection and recognition to the nuanced field of emotion analysis and the vigilant guard against deep fake content, deep learning emerges as a powerful ally in enhancing the viewer experience.

Looking to the horizon, we envisage a future where deep learning continues to unfold, wielding its transformative power to revolutionize video analysis on YouTube. A future where insights gleaned from deep learning not only enhance the viewer experience but also empower creators to forge deeper connections with their audience, crafting content that resonates on a profound level.

As we close this chapter, we hold a vision of a future rich with potential, a future where deep learning stands as a beacon of innovation, guiding us toward a more insightful, powerful, and transformative landscape in video analysis. It is a future ripe with opportunities, a future where deep learning not only shapes the world of video analysis but also redefines the boundaries of what is possible, promising a journey of discovery that is as expansive as it is exciting. It is a future we step into with anticipation, ready to embrace the myriad opportunities that lie ahead, as deep learning continues to redefine the contours of video analysis on YouTube, promising a narrative that is as rich, diverse, and vibrant as the platform itself.

Chapter 14
Virtual Reality (VR) and AI in YouTube

Virtual Reality (VR) and Artificial Intelligence (AI) are two transformative technologies that have the potential to revolutionize the YouTube experience. VR provides immersive and interactive virtual environments, while AI brings intelligence and automation to various aspects of content creation and consumption. In this chapter, we will explore the convergence of VR and AI technologies and discuss their impact on YouTube. We will delve into the role of AI in VR content creation, video editing, analytics, simulations, navigation, chatbots, and environment generation. Additionally, we will examine the ethical considerations and challenges that arise from the integration of AI and VR in the YouTube landscape. Finally, we will discuss the future of VR and AI in YouTube, including emerging trends and predictions.

Today, we see the convergence of Virtual Reality (VR) and Artificial Intelligence (AI) technologies, opening up new possibilities for immersive and intelligent experiences on YouTube. The combination of VR's ability to transport users to virtual worlds and AI's capability to enhance and automate various processes creates a powerful synergy that can transform the way we create and consume content.

The integration of VR and AI in YouTube holds immense potential to revolutionize the platform. VR can provide users with immersive and interactive experiences, while AI can enhance efficiency, personalization, and user engagement. The combination of these technologies can create unforgettable experiences, opening up new avenues for content creators and providing viewers with unique and tailored experiences.

AI-powered tools are revolutionizing VR content creation by enabling creators to design and develop immersive experiences more efficiently. AI algorithms can assist in generating lifelike environments, realistic simulations, and dynamic narratives. These tools empower creators to push the boundaries of VR content creation and create immersive experiences that captivate and engage viewers.

AI brings automation and efficiency to the VR content production process. By leveraging AI algorithms for tasks such as automating labor-intensive processes, optimizing workflows, and enhancing creativity, creators can spend more time on ideation and storytelling. AI-driven tools enable creators to streamline their production pipelines and unlock their full creative potential, resulting in innovative and compelling VR experiences on YouTube.

AI-driven algorithms can adapt VR content to individual viewers, enhancing customization and personalization. By analyzing user preferences, behavior, and contextual data, AI algorithms can dynamically adjust VR content, leading to more engaging and personalized experiences. This level of customization enables creators to cater to diverse audiences and ensures that each viewer has a unique and tailored VR experience on YouTube.

VR video editing and post-production can be time-consuming and complex due to the 360-degree nature of VR content. AI algorithms can automate tasks such as stitching together multiple video streams, reducing the manual effort required to create seamless VR experiences. These algorithms analyze video frames, detect inconsistencies, and apply image correction techniques to ensure smooth transitions and immersive viewing experiences.

AI algorithms play a crucial role in improving the quality and realism of VR content through post-production techniques. By leveraging computer vision and deep learning, AI algorithms can remove noise, enhance colors, and refine renderings to create visually stunning VR experiences. These algorithms enable creators to deliver high-quality content that immerses viewers in realistic virtual worlds and captivates their senses.

AI-powered editing tools enhance the editing process by automating routine tasks and improving productivity. These tools analyze video content, identify key scenes, and suggest edits based on predefined criteria or user preferences. By reducing manual editing efforts, AI empowers creators to focus on storytelling and creativity, accelerating the content production cycle and enabling them to produce immersive VR videos more efficiently.

AI algorithms can analyze user behavior and engagement in VR videos, providing creators with valuable insights. These algorithms track user interactions, such as head movements, gaze tracking, and hand gestures, to understand user engagement and preferences. By analyzing this data, creators can optimize their content, improve user experience, and tailor their VR experiences to better meet the expectations and demands of their audience.

AI-powered analytics tools enable creators to measure key performance metrics and optimize their VR content strategy. By analyzing data such as watch time, engagement, and audience retention, AI algorithms provide actionable insights that help creators identify successful content and refine their strategies. This data-driven approach empowers creators to make informed decisions, adapt to viewer preferences, and maximize the impact of their VR content on YouTube.

AI-driven insights can guide creators in improving user experience and optimizing content recommendations in VR. By analyzing user data, AI algorithms can provide personalized recommendations, suggest relevant VR experiences, and enhance user engagement. Creators can leverage these insights to refine their content, tailor recommendations, and create captivating VR experiences that resonate with their audience on YouTube.

AI and VR technologies can be combined to create realistic simulations that facilitate training in various industries. From medical simulations to flight training, AI algorithms analyze data and simulate real-world scenarios, providing users with an immersive and interactive training environment. These simulations enable users to practice skills, build expertise, and enhance learning outcomes within a safe and controlled VR setting.

AI-powered VR training offers personalized and adaptive learning experiences. By analyzing user performance, AI algorithms can provide real-time feedback, adapt difficulty levels, and tailor training programs to individual needs. This personalized approach enhances learning outcomes, accelerates skill development, and enables users to master complex tasks more effectively and efficiently.

AI-driven VR simulations have the potential to revolutionize learning and training across industries. From healthcare to education and beyond, these simulations enable immersive and cost-effective training experiences. AI algorithms continuously improve simulation accuracy, realism, and interactivity, expanding the application of VR simulations in industries where experiential learning is crucial.

AI technologies enhance VR navigation and user interaction by providing intuitive interfaces and gesture recognition capabilities. Natural Language Processing (NLP) algorithms enable voice commands and conversational interactions in VR environments, while gesture recognition algorithms interpret hand movements for seamless interaction. These AI-powered technologies create intuitive and immersive user experiences in VR.

AI algorithms can address challenges related to user comfort and motion sickness in VR experiences. By analyzing user behavior, AI can adapt VR content to minimize discomfort, such as adjusting frame rates or optimizing visual effects. AI enhances user comfort and reduces motion sickness, making VR experiences more enjoyable and accessible to a wider audience on YouTube.

AI-powered VR controllers and interfaces contribute to a seamless user experience by utilizing advanced motion tracking and haptic feedback algorithms. These technologies enable precise and intuitive interactions, enhancing user immersion and engagement. As AI continues to advance, VR controllers and interfaces will become more sophisticated, enabling even more natural and immersive user experiences on YouTube.

AI-driven chatbots and virtual assistants enhance interactivity and engagement in VR environments. These AI-powered conversational agents can provide users with real-time assistance, answer questions, and guide them through virtual experiences. Chatbots and virtual assistants in VR act as personal guides and companions, enriching the user experience and enhancing immersion.

Immersive AI interactions, such as natural language understanding and gesture recognition, enhance user engagement and interactivity in VR. AI algorithms enable users to communicate with virtual characters, objects, or environments, creating a more immersive and interactive user experience. These immersive AI interactions break down barriers and foster a sense of presence in VR environments.

AI chatbots can act as personal guides and companions in VR experiences, providing users with contextualized information and assistance. These chatbots can adapt to individual preferences, make recommendations, and offer personalized guidance, enhancing the overall VR experience. Creators can leverage AI chatbots to provide users with customized support, improve navigation, and create more engaging and memorable VR experiences on YouTube.

AI algorithms have the capacity to generate lifelike and immersive VR environments, expanding the creative possibilities for content creators. These algorithms analyze data, such as image and video datasets, to generate virtual worlds that mimic real-world settings or push the boundaries of imagination. AI-generated VR environments enable creators to transport viewers to captivating and visually stunning virtual landscapes.

AI-generated content allows for dynamic and customizable VR experiences. AI algorithms can generate content that adapts to user input, creating unique and personalized VR narratives on the fly. This dynamic content generation enables creators to offer customizable VR experiences, giving viewers agency and allowing them to shape their own virtual adventures on YouTube.

AI's ability to analyze and generate content opens up new avenues for VR narratives and storytelling. AI algorithms can assist creators in crafting compelling storylines, generating interactive characters, and dynamically adapting narratives based on user preferences and interactions. The fusion of AI and VR presents creators with endless creative possibilities, allowing them to push the boundaries of immersive storytelling on YouTube.

The integration of AI in VR presents ethical considerations, such as potential risks and biases. Creators and developers must ensure that AI algorithms do not adversely affect users or perpetuate biases or discriminatory behavior. Robust testing, diverse training data, and ongoing monitoring are crucial to addressing these risks and creating inclusive and responsible AI-driven VR experiences on YouTube.

AI-powered VR experiences rely on user data, raising concerns about privacy and data protection. Creators and platforms must adhere to strict privacy policies, implement adequate security measures, and obtain user consent for data collection and usage. Data anonymization, encryption, and transparency are essential in ensuring the responsible and ethical integration of AI and VR on YouTube.

The integration of AI and VR in YouTube requires creators and platforms to navigate the ethical landscape diligently. Open dialogue, collaboration, and adherence to ethical guidelines are crucial in promoting responsible AI-driven VR experiences. Regular audits, diversity in development teams, and robust testing are essential steps toward creating an inclusive, safe, and ethical environment for immersive content on YouTube.

The future of VR and AI in YouTube is characterized by emerging trends and advancements. Technologies like augmented reality, mixed reality, and natural language processing will continue to push the boundaries of immersive experiences. The integration of AI will enable even more personalized, intelligent, and interactive content on YouTube, creating a future where creators and viewers can seamlessly connect in immersive virtual worlds.

The full potential of AI in creating immersive and transformative VR experiences on YouTube is yet to be fully realized. By harnessing AI's capabilities, creators can craft content that captivates, educates, and inspires viewers on a whole new level. AI-driven content generation, intelligent recommendations, and interactive VR experiences will shape the way creators produce and viewers consume content on YouTube in the future.

Looking ahead, we can anticipate several predictions for the future of VR and AI integration in YouTube content creation and consumption. AI algorithms will become increasingly sophisticated, enabling creators to automate various processes, deliver hyper-personalized recommendations, and create immersive experiences that blur the line between virtual and physical realities. As VR and AI continue to evolve, YouTube will evolve as a platform, offering creators and viewers a dynamic and transformative content ecosystem.

As VR and AI technologies continue to evolve, the potential for creating unforgettable experiences on YouTube is limitless. By harnessing the power of AI in VR content creation, editing, analytics, simulations, navigation, chatbots, and immersive environments, creators can deliver unparalleled immersive content to their audiences. The ethical considerations and challenges that come with AI and VR integration must also be addressed to ensure a responsible and inclusive future for YouTube. With ongoing advancements and innovation in these fields, the future of VR and AI in YouTube holds great promise for creators and viewers alike.

Chapter 15
Predictive Analytics for Content Planning

Today, YouTube has become a highly competitive platform where creators constantly strive to capture their audience's attention and stay ahead of trends. In this chapter, we will explore how predictive analytics can play a crucial role in content planning on YouTube. By leveraging data-driven insights, creators can gain a competitive edge by predicting trends, understanding their audience's preferences, and optimizing their content strategies. We will delve into the benefits and applications of predictive analytics in YouTube content planning, and how it can revolutionize the way creators approach their content creation strategies.

Data-driven insights provide creators with valuable information and guidance to make informed decisions regarding their content creation strategies. By leveraging predictive analytics, creators can gain a deep understanding of their audience's preferences, identify emerging trends, and optimize their content for maximum engagement. This data-driven approach enables creators to create content that resonates with their audience, increases their reach, and enhances overall performance on YouTube. We will discuss the specific benefits of using data-driven insights in content planning, from increasing audience engagement to staying ahead of the competition, and how it can propel creators to new heights of success on YouTube.

To harness the power of predictive analytics, creators need to collect and analyze relevant data. This data can include audience demographics, viewer behavior, engagement metrics, and content performance. We will explore different methods of data collection, such as YouTube Analytics, third-party analytics tools, and surveys, and discuss the importance of quality data in enabling accurate predictive analytics. Additionally, we will emphasize the significance of data integrity, privacy, and security, and provide insights into best practices for data collection and storage on YouTube.

The sheer volume of data on YouTube can be overwhelming for creators. That's where AI tools and algorithms come in. By leveraging AI, creators can streamline the data processing and analysis process, making it more efficient and accurate. AI algorithms can assist in data cleaning, data preprocessing, and feature extraction, making it easier for creators to derive meaningful insights from the data. We will discuss popular AI tools and algorithms that can aid creators in efficient data processing, and how they can optimize the predictive analytics process for content planning.

With the increasing importance of data in content planning, data privacy and security become paramount concerns. Creators must ensure that they adhere to privacy regulations, obtain proper consent from their viewers, and employ secure data storage and handling practices. We will discuss the ethical considerations and challenges associated with data privacy and security in predictive analytics and provide guidance on how creators can navigate these concerns. By maintaining data privacy and security, creators can build trust with their audience and ensure the responsible use of data in content planning on YouTube.

One of the key advantages of predictive analytics is its ability to identify emerging trends in content consumption. By analyzing historical data and predicting future trends, creators can stay ahead of the curve and create content that resonates with their audience. We will explore how predictive analytics algorithms can identify emerging trends, from analyzing search patterns to monitoring social media buzz, and discuss how creators can leverage these insights to create timely and relevant content that captures their viewers' attention.

Understanding viewer behavior and preferences is crucial for effective content planning on YouTube. Predictive analytics allows creators to analyze patterns in viewer engagement, such as watch time, click-through rates, and viewer retention. By identifying these patterns, creators can optimize their content strategies to better align with their audience's preferences. We will discuss how predictive analytics algorithms can analyze viewer behavior and provide insights into optimal content formats, lengths, and release schedules. With this information, creators can maximize viewer engagement and create content that keeps their audience coming back for more.

Predictive analytics can uncover niche markets and untapped opportunities for creators on YouTube. By analyzing data on viewer demographics, interests, and preferences, creators can identify underserved or emerging niche markets. We will explore how predictive analytics algorithms can uncover these opportunities, from identifying niche content categories to predicting the success of new content ideas. With this information, creators can tailor their content strategies to target specific niche markets, increasing their chances of success and expanding their audience base.

Audience segmentation is crucial for effective content planning on YouTube. Predictive analytics algorithms can assist creators in segmenting their audience based on demographic, geographic, and psychographic factors. By understanding their audience's characteristics and preferences, creators can tailor their content to specific segments, increasing engagement and building a loyal audience base. We will explore how predictive analytics algorithms can identify audience segments and discuss the various factors creators should consider when segmenting their audience on YouTube.

Once creators have identified their audience segments, predictive analytics can assist in tailoring content strategies to meet the specific needs and preferences of each segment. By analyzing data on viewer behavior, engagement, and preferences, creators can create personalized content that resonates with each audience segment. We will explore how predictive analytics algorithms can provide insights into content formats, topics, and styles that appeal to specific audience segments. With this information, creators can optimize their content strategies, increase viewer engagement, and strengthen their connection with their audience on YouTube.

Personalization is key to driving engagement and viewer satisfaction on YouTube. Predictive analytics enables creators to personalize content recommendations and experiences based on audience preferences. By analyzing data on viewer behavior, past interactions, and preferences, predictive analytics algorithms can generate personalized content recommendations tailored to each viewer. We will discuss how creators can leverage predictive analytics to deliver personalized recommendations, enhance viewer satisfaction, and increase overall engagement on YouTube.

Seasonality plays a significant role in content planning on YouTube. Predictive analytics can help creators identify seasonal trends and optimize their content strategies accordingly. By analyzing historical data and predicting future trends, creators can create content that aligns with the seasonal interests and demands of their audience. We will explore how predictive analytics algorithms can identify seasonal patterns, from holiday trends to seasonal search queries, and discuss how creators can leverage these insights to optimize their content strategies and maximize viewer engagement during specific seasons.

Timeliness is crucial for successful content planning on YouTube. Predictive analytics allows creators to identify timely topics and events that are relevant to their audience. By analyzing data on trending keywords, social media conversations, and search queries, creators can stay informed about the latest trends and capitalize on them in their content planning. We will discuss how predictive analytics algorithms can identify timely topics and events, and how creators can leverage these insights to create content that resonates with their audience and captures the current cultural zeitgeist.

Trends and viewer interests are constantly evolving on YouTube. Predictive analytics enables creators to adapt their content strategies based on changing trends and viewer preferences. By monitoring data on viewer behavior, engagement metrics, and content performance, creators can identify shifts in viewer interests and adjust their content strategies accordingly. We will explore how predictive analytics algorithms can provide insights into changing trends and viewer interests, and discuss the strategies creators can employ to stay ahead of the curve and maintain the relevance and engagement of their content on YouTube.

Predictive analytics allows creators to predict video and channel performance based on historical data and audience engagement metrics. By applying predictive analytics models, creators can forecast the potential success of their videos and channels, enabling them to make informed decisions about content production and distribution. We will discuss how predictive analytics algorithms can provide insights into video and channel performance, from predicting view counts to estimating subscriber growth. With this information, creators can optimize their content strategies and maximize their chances of success on YouTube.

Predictive analytics provides creators with insights into how they can optimize their content to increase viewer engagement and reach. By analyzing data on viewer behavior, engagement metrics, and trends, creators can identify areas for improvement and make data-driven decisions about content optimization. We will explore how predictive analytics algorithms can provide insights into content formats, lengths, thumbnails, titles, and descriptions that optimize viewer engagement and increase reach. With these insights, creators can refine their content strategies, maximize viewer engagement, and grow their audience on YouTube.

A/B testing and iterative optimization are essential for refining content strategies and maximizing performance on YouTube. Predictive analytics algorithms can assist creators in conducting A/B tests and analyzing the results to make data-driven decisions about content optimization. By comparing different variations of their content, creators can identify which elements resonate best with their audience and refine their content accordingly. We will discuss how creators can leverage predictive analytics to conduct A/B tests, measure performance, and iteratively optimize their content strategies on YouTube.

Collaboration is a powerful tool in content planning on YouTube. Predictive analytics can assist creators in collaborative content planning by analyzing data and providing insights that can guide the decision-making process. By leveraging predictive analytics algorithms, creators can identify common audience segments, align content strategies, and create collaborative content that appeals to a broader audience. We will explore how creators can utilize predictive analytics to enhance collaboration, optimize content planning processes, and foster innovation on YouTube.

AI-driven tools streamline the collaboration process and optimize resource allocation in content planning. By automating tasks such as file sharing, feedback collection, and resource allocation, AI enables creators to collaborate more efficiently and effectively. We will discuss how creators can leverage AI-driven collaboration tools, such as project management software and content planning platforms, to enhance collaboration, improve productivity, and optimize resource allocation on YouTube.

Collaboration enhances content planning efficiency and fosters innovation on YouTube. By sharing insights, ideas, and resources, creators can pool their collective knowledge to create more impactful and innovative content. We will discuss how collaboration can drive content planning efficiency, spark creativity, and introduce new perspectives that can elevate the quality and reach of content on YouTube. With collaboration and predictive analytics, creators can push the boundaries of content creation and deliver exceptional experiences to their viewers.

Predictive analytics algorithms can assist creators in curating and recommending relevant content to their audience. By analyzing viewer data and preferences, creators can curate playlists, recommend related videos, and deliver personalized content experiences. We will explore how predictive analytics algorithms can provide insights into content curation and recommendation strategies, and how creators can leverage these insights to enhance user experience, increase engagement, and foster audience loyalty on YouTube.

Personalized recommendations are key to enhancing user experience and driving engagement on YouTube. Predictive analytics enables creators to deliver personalized recommendations by analyzing viewer behavior, preferences, and contextual data. By tailoring content recommendations to individual viewers, creators can provide a more relevant and engaging viewing experience. We will discuss how creators can leverage predictive analytics to personalize recommendations, increase viewer satisfaction, and foster long-term engagement on YouTube.

While content curation algorithms offer significant benefits, they also introduce ethical considerations and biases. Creators must address potential biases and ensure that content curation algorithms are fair, diverse, and inclusive. We will explore strategies for addressing biases, such as transparency in algorithms, diverse training data, and regular audits. By taking ethical considerations into account, creators can create inclusive and unbiased content curation algorithms that enhance viewer experience on YouTube.

Predictive analytics plays a fundamental role in long-term content strategy planning. By analyzing historical data, audience behavior, and industry trends, creators can develop forward-thinking strategies that align with their audience's interests and aspirations. We will discuss how predictive analytics algorithms can provide insights into long-term content strategies, from content format planning to audience expansion. With this information, creators can make informed decisions that set them on a path to long-term success on YouTube.

AI-powered tools enable creators to conduct forecasting and scenario analysis to inform long-term content planning. By utilizing predictive analytics algorithms, creators can analyze historical data, predict future trends, and model different scenarios. We will explore how creators can leverage AI-powered tools for forecasting and scenario analysis, and how these insights can guide long-term content decision-making, resource allocation, and audience expansion strategies on YouTube.

In a competitive landscape like YouTube, staying ahead of the competition is crucial for success. Predictive analytics provides creators with a data-driven advantage, enabling them to identify trends, optimize content strategies, and capture their audience's attention. We will discuss how creators can leverage predictive analytics to stay ahead of the competition, explore emerging content formats, and innovate within their niche. By staying informed and adaptive, creators can maintain a competitive edge and drive long-term growth on YouTube.

Predictive analytics enables creators to measure the return on investment (ROI) of their content planning efforts. By analyzing data on metrics such as view counts, engagement, and audience growth, creators can assess the impact and effectiveness of their content strategies. We will explore how creators can leverage predictive analytics algorithms to measure ROI, make data-driven decisions, and optimize their content planning processes to maximize the return on their investments on YouTube.

Predictive analytics provides creators with tools to evaluate the success and impact of their predictive strategies on content performance. By comparing predicted outcomes with actual results, creators can assess the accuracy and effectiveness of their predictive analytics models. We will discuss how creators can evaluate the success and impact of their predictive strategies, identify areas for improvement, and refine their content planning approaches on YouTube.

Performance evaluation is essential for continuous improvement in content planning on YouTube. By analyzing data on content performance, viewer engagement, and audience feedback, creators can gain valuable insights into their strengths and areas for improvement. We will discuss how creators can leverage performance evaluation to inform future content planning, refine content strategies, and optimize their approach to creating and delivering content on YouTube.

Predictive analytics has emerged as a transformative tool for content planning on YouTube. By harnessing the power of data-driven insights, creators can stay ahead of trends, effectively target their audience, optimize content for maximum engagement, and collaborate with other creators. Predictive analytics also facilitates long-term strategy planning and enables creators to evaluate the performance and ROI of their content planning efforts. With the continued advancements in AI and analytics, the future of content planning on YouTube will be even more informed, strategic, and successful. The integration of predictive analytics into the content planning process empowers creators to create captivating and impactful content that resonates with their audience, propelling them to new heights of success on YouTube.

Chapter 16
Advanced YouTube Analytics with AI

In this chapter, we will explore the power of advanced YouTube analytics enhanced by Artificial Intelligence (AI). We will discuss the importance of analytics in YouTube content creation, the limitations of traditional methods, and how AI can overcome these limitations to provide deep insights. Additionally, we will delve into leveraging AI for audience insights, enhancing video performance, understanding viewer behavior, driving content recommendations, harnessing AI for competitor analysis, monetization, and SEO, while also considering data privacy and ethical considerations. Lastly, we will take a glimpse into the future of AI-enhanced YouTube analytics.

Today, analytics play a vital role in understanding your audience, improving content performance, and maximizing channel growth. We will uncover the invaluable insights that YouTube analytics provide to creators in driving meaningful and impactful content strategies.

Traditional analytics methods often fall short in capturing the complex and nuanced data needed to fully comprehend audience behavior. We will discuss these limitations and how AI can bridge the gap by offering cutting-edge analytics capabilities.

AI has revolutionized the way we analyze data, enabling us to uncover patterns, predict future outcomes, and provide real-time insights. We will explore how AI enhances YouTube analytics and opens new possibilities for creators.

Understanding your audience is crucial for creating targeted content. We will discuss how AI-driven segmentation and profiling tools can help you identify different audience segments and tailor your content to meet their needs.

AI-powered predictive analytics enables you to forecast audience preferences and trends, helping you plan your content strategy effectively. We will explore how AI algorithms can analyze vast amounts of audience data to provide actionable insights.

Real-time audience engagement monitoring allows you to assess the impact of your content as it unfolds. We will discuss how AI can help you monitor audience sentiment, measure engagement, and make data-driven decisions to optimize your content in real-time.

AI-driven video performance metrics provide deeper insights into the performance of your videos. We will explore how AI can analyze engagement metrics, such as watch time, likes, and comments, to help you identify areas of improvement and optimize your videos for maximum impact.

A/B testing is a powerful method for optimizing video performance. We will discuss how AI can automate A/B testing, allowing you to evaluate different video versions, thumbnails, titles, and descriptions to determine what resonates best with your audience.

AI can assist in optimizing videos by analyzing viewer preferences, tags, and metadata. We will explore AI-driven video optimization techniques that can help you improve your video discoverability, increase watch time, and drive organic growth.

AI can analyze viewing patterns and trends to provide insights on how your audience interacts with your content. We will discuss how AI algorithms can identify peak viewing times, binge-watching behavior, and content preferences, empowering you to create targeted and engaging content.

Understanding viewer engagement is essential for creating captivating content. We will explore how AI can analyze viewer behavior, such as pause rates and rewatches, to assess audience engagement and guide your content creation strategies.

AI algorithms can identify audience retention and drop-off points within your videos. We will discuss how these insights can help you identify areas where viewers lose interest, allowing you to make informed decisions for content improvement and keeping your audience engaged.

AI-powered content recommendation engines can suggest personalized videos to viewers based on their browsing behavior, preferences, and demographics. We will explore how AI can enhance the viewer experience by delivering relevant and engaging content, increasing viewer retention.

AI algorithms, such as collaborative filtering and content-based filtering, can uncover related videos that are likely to interest your viewers. We will discuss how AI-driven content recommendation systems can boost viewer engagement and extend their time on your channel.

Utilizing AI to recommend videos during critical retention points can be a game-changer. We will explore how AI can analyze viewer behavior and retention analytics to identify optimal video insertion points, ultimately improving viewer retention and session duration.

AI-driven competitive intelligence tools provide valuable insights into your competitors' strategies and performance. We will discuss how AI can help you analyze their content, engagement metrics, and audience demographics to gain a competitive edge.

AI can track and analyze your competitors' video performance, allowing you to benchmark your own content against theirs. We will explore how AI can provide you with actionable insights to improve your own videos and outperform your competitors.

By leveraging AI insights, you can identify untapped content opportunities, optimize your strategies, and stay ahead of your competitors. We will discuss how AI can help you uncover trends, analyze gaps in the market, and develop a competitive advantage on YouTube.

AI can optimize ad placements to maximize revenue while ensuring a positive user experience. We will explore how AI algorithms can analyze viewer behavior, ad performance, and contextual data to deliver targeted and effective ad placements.

AI-powered predictive analytics can forecast ad performance and revenue potential. We will discuss how AI can help you identify optimal ad placement strategies, pricing models, and target demographics to maximize your ad revenue on YouTube.

AI algorithms can recommend sponsored content that aligns with your viewers' preferences, ensuring a seamless integration of branded content into your YouTube channel. We will explore how AI can help you select the right sponsors and create compelling branded content for your audience.

AI can revolutionize keyword research and analysis, enabling you to identify high-impact keywords and optimize your videos for better search rankings. We will discuss how AI can help you uncover hidden keyword opportunities, analyze search trends, and improve your video SEO.

AI algorithms can generate compelling video titles and descriptions that attract viewers and improve search visibility. We will explore how AI can guide you in crafting engaging titles and optimized descriptions that drive organic traffic to your videos.

AI can provide valuable insights into channel growth strategies based on analytics data. We will discuss how AI algorithms can analyze subscriber behavior, demographics, and engagement metrics to help you refine your content strategy, promote subscriber growth, and optimize your channel's performance.

Data privacy is crucial when utilizing AI for analytics. We will discuss privacy concerns associated with AI-powered YouTube analytics and explore best practices for safeguarding user data and ensuring compliance with privacy regulations.

Transparency is key in data handling for AI analytics. We will discuss how to communicate your data handling practices clearly to viewers, acquire consent, and provide options for users to control data collection and analysis.

Ethics play a vital role in AI-powered analytics. We will explore ethical considerations in collecting and analyzing data, ensuring fairness, avoiding biases, and using AI responsibly to respect viewer trust and maintain the integrity of the YouTube platform.

Cutting-edge technologies, such as machine learning, natural language processing, and computer vision, are shaping the future of YouTube analytics with AI. We will discuss these emerging technologies and their potential to revolutionize how creators analyze and optimize their content.

AI is continuously evolving, offering new possibilities in data interpretation. We will explore how AI can enhance data visualization, pattern recognition, and predictive modeling, enabling creators to extract deeper insights from their YouTube analytics.

In the next section, we will discuss our predictions for the future of AI-enhanced YouTube analytics. We will explore how AI will continue to advance, allowing creators to gain even more comprehensive and actionable insights to drive the success of their channels.

By leveraging AI for advanced YouTube analytics, creators can unlock the full potential of their content, understand their audience at a deeper level, optimize video performance, and drive channel growth. This chapter will equip creators with the knowledge and tools to harness the power of AI in their YouTube analytics journey.

Chapter 17
The Future of AI and YouTube

In this chapter, we will embark on an exciting journey into the future of AI and YouTube, exploring the groundbreaking possibilities that arise from the integration of AI technology. With the evolving landscape of AI in the digital era, we can witness its profound impact on YouTube content creation and management. Looking ahead, the future possibilities of AI in YouTube are boundless, promising enhanced viewer experiences, streamlined production processes, and ethical considerations. Join us as we delve into each step of this chapter and uncover the transformative potential AI holds for creators and the platform as a whole.

The digital era has brought about immense advancements in AI technology, revolutionizing various industries. With YouTube at the forefront of content creation and consumption, the integration of AI has the power to reshape the platform's landscape. In this section, we will set the stage by exploring the evolving landscape of AI and its impact on YouTube content creation and management. By understanding the past and present, we can better grasp the scope of possibilities that lie ahead.

Today, AI is rapidly transforming numerous fields, such as healthcare, finance, and transportation. As we see AI-driven innovations shaping industries across the globe, it becomes evident that the digital landscape is ever-evolving. This section will explore the evolution of AI, highlighting key milestones and breakthroughs that have paved the way for its integration in YouTube.

The integration of AI in YouTube has already begun to transform the content creation and management processes. From AI-generated scripting and storyboarding to real-time editing assistance, creators now have access to powerful tools that enhance their creative workflows. This section will delve into the impact AI has on YouTube content creation and management, unveiling the potential of smarter workflows, increased efficiency, and improved content quality.

The future possibilities of AI in YouTube are truly exciting, promising innovation and growth. As we peer into the horizon, we can anticipate AI-driven virtual influencers, enhanced viewer interaction, and even AI-hosted channels. However, with these possibilities come ethical considerations that require careful thought and collaboration. This section will explore the potential directions that AI may take in YouTube, giving us a glimpse into what the future holds for creators and viewers alike.

With AI technology advancing at a rapid pace, content creators now have access to powerful tools that streamline and enhance the content creation and editing processes. In this section, we will explore how AI can generate video scripts and storyboards, provide real-time editing assistance, and integrate virtual reality and augmented reality experiences, revolutionizing the way creators bring their ideas to life.

Traditionally, crafting compelling video scripts and storyboards required hours of laborious work. However, with AI-generated scripting and storyboarding, creators can now leverage the power of machine learning algorithms to generate creative and engaging narratives effortlessly. This section will dive into the possibilities and benefits of AI-generated video scripting and storyboarding, highlighting the seamless integration of AI technology into the content creation process.

Editing is an essential part of the content creation process, requiring precision and creativity. AI technology can now provide real-time editing assistance, facilitating seamless editing workflows and enhancing the final product. Creators can leverage AI algorithms to refine their edits, enhance visual effects, and automate repetitive tasks. This section will explore the application of real-time AI-based editing and production assistance, empowering creators to produce high-quality content more efficiently.

Virtual reality (VR) and augmented reality (AR) have gained significant traction in recent years, providing immersive experiences for viewers. By integrating AI-driven VR and AR, creators can transport their audience into virtual worlds, blurring the lines between the digital and physical realms. This section will uncover the potential of AI-driven VR and AR integration in YouTube, exploring the creation of interactive and captivating experiences that redefine viewer engagement.

In a fascinating development, AI technology has given rise to virtual influencers and personalities, blurring the boundaries between human and machine. This section will explore the emergence of AI-hosted channels, considering the ethical considerations that arise and contemplating the future of AI-driven content delivery and fan engagement.

AI-powered virtual influencers have taken the social media landscape by storm, captivating audiences with their flawless appearance and charismatic personalities. This section will delve into the world of AI-powered virtual influencers, considering their impact on the influencer marketing industry and the evolving dynamics between creators, virtual personalities, and their viewers.

With the emergence of AI-hosted channels and virtual influencers, new ethical considerations come to light. Questions surrounding authenticity, transparency, and the manipulation of user perceptions arise, necessitating a careful examination of the consequences and implications of AI-hosted channels. This section will explore the ethical considerations surrounding AI-hosted channels and the need for responsible AI practices.

As AI technology continues to evolve, the future of AI-driven content delivery and fan engagement holds endless possibilities. This section will explore the potential for AI-driven recommendations, personalized fan interactions, and even AI-powered video game integration. By examining the ever-expanding boundaries of AI and its impact on content delivery, we can glimpse the future landscape of YouTube and the exciting experiences it holds for creators and viewers.

AI's capabilities extend beyond content creation and editing, offering predictive insights that empower creators to plan and produce content more strategically. In this section, we will explore how AI can identify content trends and demands, predict audience engagement, and streamline production processes.

Content creators must stay ahead of the curve, understanding the latest trends and demands to captivate their audience effectively. AI technology can analyze vast amounts of data, such as search trends and social media chatter, providing creators with actionable insights into content trends and demands. This section will explore how AI-driven algorithms can empower creators to identify trending topics, optimize their content strategy, and engage with their audience more effectively.

Understanding audience engagement is crucial for creating content that resonates with viewers. AI-based predictive analytics algorithms can analyze historical data and audience behavior to forecast audience engagement, helping creators plan their content strategy more effectively. This section will uncover the power of AI-driven predictive analytics in gauging audience interest, enhancing engagement, and ensuring the success of content produced on YouTube.

AI can streamline the production process by optimizing planning and scheduling workflows. By analyzing historical data, production timelines, and resource availability, AI algorithms can recommend optimized production plans, reducing bottlenecks and increasing efficiency. This section will examine the potential of AI-driven planning and scheduling in content creation, enhancing the overall productivity and quality of YouTube channels.

AI technology opens doors to interactive and immersive experiences for viewers. In this section, we will explore how AI can power interactive videos, provide natural language processing for enhanced voice commands and search, and deliver AI-driven recommendations for 360-degree and VR content, ultimately enhancing viewer interaction and immersion.

Interactive videos and choose your own adventure experiences have become increasingly popular, allowing viewers to actively participate in the content they consume. AI technology plays a crucial role in delivering seamless and immersive interactive experiences, enabling creators to captivate their audience. This section will explore the power of AI in driving interactive videos, enhancing viewer agency, and revolutionizing the way viewers engage with content on YouTube.

With the rise of voice-controlled devices and virtual assistants, natural language processing (NLP) has become a critical technology in delivering enhanced voice commands and search capabilities. AI-driven NLP algorithms can understand and interpret user queries, enabling more conversational and accurate interactions. This section will uncover the potential of AI-driven NLP in YouTube, improving user experiences and expanding the possibilities for voice-controlled content consumption.

360-degree videos and VR content have the power to transport viewers into immersive and captivating experiences. AI algorithms can analyze viewer behavior and preferences to deliver personalized recommendations for 360-degree and VR content, enhancing viewer engagement and satisfaction. This section will explore the capabilities of AI-driven recommendations, enabling creators to connect viewers with the most relevant and enjoyable 360-degree and VR experiences.

The global nature of YouTube necessitates the accessibility of content to diverse audiences worldwide. In this section, we will explore how AI can provide real-time video translation for global audiences, automate subtitling and captioning processes, and optimize multilingual content, enabling creators to bridge language barriers and expand their reach.

Video translation is crucial for reaching global audiences, and AI can provide real-time translations, removing language barriers and expanding content accessibility. This section will discuss the power of AI in facilitating real-time video translations, empowering creators to engage with viewers around the world and create truly inclusive content on YouTube.

Subtitling and captioning enhance accessibility and improve viewer experiences. AI-powered automated subtitling and captioning tools can accurately transcribe spoken words and synchronize them with video content. This section will explore the benefits of AI-driven automated subtitling and captioning, enabling creators to efficiently deliver their message to audiences with hearing impairments or language preferences.

YouTube creators often produce content in multiple languages to cater to a diverse audience. AI algorithms can detect language patterns within videos, segment content by language, and optimize metadata for better search visibility. This section will uncover the power of AI in language detection and multilingual content optimization, assisting creators in effectively engaging with their audiences in different regions and languages.

With the expanding YouTube community comes the need for effective content moderation and community management. In this section, we will explore how AI can power automated content moderation, detect and combat toxic user behavior, and provide AI-driven insights for effective community management, fostering a safe and vibrant community for creators and viewers.

Content moderation is essential for maintaining a safe and positive environment on YouTube. AI algorithms can analyze videos and automatically flag content that violates community guidelines, minimizing manual intervention and expediting the moderation process. This section will discuss the impact of AI-powered automated content moderation, ensuring that YouTube remains a platform where creators can express themselves while upholding the values of the community.

Toxic user behavior, such as harassment and hate speech, can harm the YouTube community and discourage creators. AI-driven algorithms can detect patterns of toxic behavior, helping creators identify and address these issues promptly. This section will explore the capabilities of AI in detecting and combating toxic user behavior, fostering a more inclusive and respectful YouTube community.

Effective community management is crucial for fostering a vibrant and engaged YouTube community. AI algorithms can analyze community engagement and sentiment, providing creators with insights to increase viewer participation and strengthen their connection with their audience. This section will uncover the power of AI-driven insights in effective community management, enabling creators to nurture and grow their community on YouTube.

The integration of AI and blockchain technology holds immense potential for YouTube, ensuring a transparent and secure environment for creators and viewers. In this section, we will explore how AI can enable content copyright protection and plagiarism detection, facilitate transparent and secure content distribution through blockchain integration, and empower AI-driven content licensing and royalty management.

Content creators face the persistent challenge of copyright infringement and plagiarism. AI algorithms can detect and prevent unauthorized use of copyrighted content, ensuring that creators' intellectual property rights are protected. This section will discuss the capabilities of AI in content copyright protection and plagiarism detection, providing creators with the tools to safeguard their work and promote a fair environment on YouTube.

Blockchain technology offers transparency and security in content distribution, revolutionizing the way creators monetize and distribute their work. AI can facilitate the integration of blockchain in YouTube, ensuring transparent royalty payments and secure content distribution mechanisms. This section will explore the potential of AI-driven blockchain integration, empowering creators with greater control over their content and fostering trust within the YouTube ecosystem.

Content licensing and royalty management processes can be complex and time-consuming. AI algorithms can streamline these processes by automating licensing agreements, tracking content usage, and facilitating accurate and transparent royalty payments. This section will delve into the power of AI-driven content licensing and royalty management, empowering creators to monetize their work efficiently and fairly.

AI technology offers new avenues for monetization and brand collaboration for YouTube creators. In this section, we will explore how AI enables dynamic ad insertion and personalized ad targeting, powers AI-driven influencer marketing and brand collaborations, and maximizes revenue through AI-driven YouTube channel optimization.

AI algorithms can analyze viewer preferences, demographics, and online behavior to deliver dynamic and personalized ad placements. This section will discuss the possibilities of AI-driven dynamic ad insertion and personalized ad targeting, enhancing the effectiveness of ad campaigns, improving viewer experiences, and generating increased revenue for creators.

Influencer marketing has become a powerful tool for creators to monetize their channels. AI algorithms can identify suitable brand partnerships, matching creators with brands that align with their content and target audience. This section will explore the potential of AI-powered influencer marketing and brand collaboration, empowering creators to build meaningful and authentic partnerships that resonate with their viewers.

Optimizing YouTube channels for maximum revenue requires careful analysis and strategy. AI-driven analytics can provide creators with insights into revenue generation opportunities, channel monetization strategies, and subscriber growth tactics. This section will uncover the power of AI in optimizing YouTube channels for revenue, helping creators maximize their earnings and achieve sustainable growth.

As AI technology continues to advance, ethical considerations become increasingly important. In this section, we will address bias and ethical concerns in AI algorithms, discuss strategies to ensure user privacy in AI-enhanced YouTube experiences, and explore collaborative efforts for developing ethical AI practices that promote fairness, transparency, and accountability.

AI algorithms, while powerful, can be susceptible to biases and ethical concerns. This section will delve into the importance of detecting and addressing biases in AI algorithms, promoting fairness and inclusivity in content recommendations, moderation processes, and user interactions on YouTube.

User privacy is a critical aspect of AI-enhanced experiences on YouTube. Creators and platform providers must adopt privacy-centric practices, ensuring user data is handled responsibly and transparently. This section will explore the measures creators can take to protect user privacy while utilizing AI technology, guaranteeing a safe and trustworthy environment for viewers.

Building trust and promoting ethical AI practices on YouTube require collaborative efforts from creators, platform providers, and regulatory bodies. This section will discuss the importance of collaboration in developing ethical AI practices, fostering transparency, accountability, and responsible AI use on YouTube.

As we conclude this chapter, the future possibilities of AI in YouTube are tantalizing. The integration of AI technology promises enhanced content creation and editing, the emergence of AI-hosted channels, predictive content planning and production, enhanced viewer interaction and immersion, automated video translation and subtitling, AI-enhanced content moderation and community management, the integration of AI and blockchain, enhanced monetization and brand partnership, and ethical considerations that shape the future landscape of YouTube.

Chapter 17 opens doors to a new era of YouTube, where creators can harness the power of AI to create captivating content, engage with their audience, and optimize their channel's success. As AI continues to evolve and new possibilities emerge, creators must navigate the ethical landscape, ensuring transparency, fairness, and respect for user privacy. Join us as we explore the limitless potential of AI and its exciting future in YouTube.

Chapter 18
AI for Thumbnail Creation

Captivating and visually appealing thumbnails can make all the difference in attracting viewers. In this chapter, we will explore the power of AI in thumbnail creation, ensuring that creators can optimize their visual representation and increase the click-through rate of their videos. We will delve into the innovative techniques and tools that AI offers, empowering creators to create compelling thumbnails that captivate their audience's attention.

Thumbnails are the visual gateway to your videos, drawing viewers in and enticing them to click. We will explore the significance of captivating thumbnails in enhancing viewer engagement and boosting the click-through rate of your videos. YouTube's algorithm considers various factors when recommending videos, including thumbnail relevance and appeal. We will discuss how thumbnails can impact your video's visibility and discoverability on the platform.

Crafting a thumbnail that captivates viewers involves a harmonious blend of creativity, aesthetics, and relevance. This intricate art form is designed to spark curiosity and encourage viewers to engage with your videos. To achieve this, one can leverage the power of AI algorithms, which stand ready to dissect the visual elements of your videos meticulously, pinpointing those key frames that hold the potential to be transformed into captivating thumbnails.

Delving further, we find that AI-driven image recognition and analysis come into play, offering assistance in cherry-picking the most visually appealing and pertinent thumbnail options. This process is not just about selecting an image; it is about choosing a visual representation that encapsulates the essence of the video, a snapshot that promises viewers content that is both engaging and relevant.

Yet, the role of AI extends beyond the visual realm, venturing into the complex world of human emotions. Here, AI showcases its prowess in analyzing viewers' emotional responses to thumbnails, a task achieved through meticulous scrutiny of facial expressions and other non-verbal cues, thereby identifying the emotions that are most likely to foster engagement. This emotional resonance is a powerful tool, enabling creators to forge a deeper connection with their target audience, crafting thumbnails that not only catch the eye but also resonate on a more profound, emotional level.

As we venture further into this topic, we encounter the dynamic world of AI-powered A/B testing, a realm where different thumbnail variations are not just created but also analyzed for their performance. This analytical approach, grounded in data, allows for an optimization strategy that promises to enhance click-through rates and foster greater engagement. Through intelligent analysis of viewer data, AI facilitates a strategy that is both dynamic and responsive, adapting to viewer preferences and trends, and ensuring that your thumbnail strategy remains not just relevant but also highly effective.

In thworld of AI-enhanced thumbnail creation, we witness a marriage of art and science, a union that promises to revolutionize the way we approach thumbnail creation. Through the lens of AI, we are offered tools that are both powerful and insightful, guiding creators in crafting thumbnails that are not just visually appealing but also emotionally resonant, promising a viewer experience that is both enriching and engaging. This is the frontier of thumbnail creation, a space where creativity meets technology, offering unprecedented opportunities for engagement and success.

AI-driven thumbnail generators leverage advanced algorithms to create compelling and visually appealing thumbnails automatically. We will discuss the capabilities of these tools and how they can help you save time and create professional-looking thumbnails effortlessly.

AI technology can enable customized thumbnail creation based on viewer preferences, demographics, and browsing behavior. We will explore how AI-powered tools can help you personalize thumbnails to suit your target audience, enhancing viewer engagement and enticing more clicks.

AI stands as a potent collaborator, ready to join forces with human artists to craft thumbnails that are not only stunning but also unique. This collaboration, which we will delve into, marries human creativity with AI insights, fostering the creation of visually striking thumbnails that demand attention on YouTube. This process is further enriched by maintaining a consistency in thumbnail design and branding, a strategy that fosters instant content recognition. We will navigate through the best practices that encourage the incorporation of consistent branding elements and styles into your thumbnails, thereby establishing a robust visual identity on YouTube.

As we forge ahead, we find that the allure of compelling visuals and effective call-to-action elements in thumbnails cannot be understated. These elements hold the power to entice viewers, encouraging them to engage with your videos. Our discussion will encompass the optimal use of visuals, fonts, and overlay text, strategies designed to create thumbnails that not only captivate but also drive viewership. This journey through the world of thumbnail creation also takes us through the diverse landscape of content genres, each demanding a unique thumbnail strategy. From gaming and vlogging to educational content, we will delineate the best practices that ensure your thumbnails not only align with your content but also resonate deeply with your target audience.

In this dynamic environment, the role of analytics emerges as a powerful tool, offering insights into thumbnail performance through a data-driven lens. We will dissect the ways to harness analytics tools effectively, guiding you in making informed decisions that optimize your thumbnails based on solid data. This optimization is not a one-time event but a continuous journey, requiring an iterative approach grounded in viewer feedback, A/B testing, and meticulous data analysis. As we delve deeper, we will unravel strategies that promise to refine your thumbnail strategy over time, adapting to the ever-evolving YouTube trends and viewer preferences.

As we approach the end of this journey, we find ourselves in the realm of authenticity and relevance, two pillars that stand tall in the world of thumbnail creation. Our discussion will emphasize the critical role of accurate content representation through thumbnails, steering clear of misleading or deceptive practices that can erode viewer trust. This path also leads us to the sensitive territory of content that requires a delicate touch, demanding ethical practices in thumbnail creation to respect viewer sensitivities.

As we near the conclusion, we will touch upon the legal landscape surrounding thumbnail creation, emphasizing adherence to copyright and fair use guidelines. This involves a deep understanding of the principles of fair use, knowledge of how to obtain necessary permissions, and the best practices for using copyrighted images responsibly. Looking forward, we see the horizon of AI technology, continuously advancing and promising to revolutionize thumbnail creation and optimization through emerging techniques such as object recognition, sentiment analysis, and image synthesis.

Finally, we stand on the cusp of a future where AI promises to usher in an era of customized and personalized thumbnails, crafted meticulously at scale.

We will envision the future possibilities of AI-driven thumbnail customization, a world where AI algorithms sift through vast amounts of viewer data, crafting thumbnails that are not just personalized but also deeply aligned with individual preferences and engagement patterns. This is the future of thumbnail creation, a landscape rich with potential, promising a viewer experience that is both enriching and deeply personal.

In the future, AI may seamlessly collaborate with human designers, enabling creators to leverage the creativity and expertise of both AI and human artists. We will explore the potential of AI-assisted thumbnail collaboration to deliver visually stunning and highly engaging thumbnails that captivate viewers' attention.

As we conclude this chapter, AI-powered thumbnail creation opens up a world of possibilities for YouTube creators. By leveraging AI technology, creators can craft captivating thumbnails that entice viewers and maximize engagement. The future promises even greater advancements in AI image recognition, customization, and collaboration, further enhancing the visual appeal and performance of YouTube thumbnails. Join us as we embrace the power of AI in thumbnail creation and position your videos for success on YouTube.

Chapter 19
AI-Driven Content Scheduling

There is a high importance that scheduling plays a crucial role in optimizing the reach and engagement of your YouTube videos. In this chapter, we will explore how Artificial Intelligence (AI) can revolutionize content scheduling for creators. We will discuss the benefits of AI in optimizing content release timing, explore AI-powered algorithms for determining the best scheduling strategies, and delve into data-driven insights that can enhance your content distribution strategy. With AI-driven content scheduling, creators can maximize their potential audience reach, increase viewership, and optimize content performance.

At the heart of this revolution lies smart content scheduling, a concept grounded in the understanding that the timing of content release carries substantial weight in determining its reach and engagement. We will navigate the intricacies of how intelligent scheduling can amplify your video's visibility, extending its reach to a broader audience while fostering enhanced viewer engagement. This journey takes us deeper into the workings of the YouTube algorithm, a complex entity that considers a myriad of factors including the freshness of content and the engagement it garners in the initial hours post-release. Here, we will dissect how AI stands as a potent tool, capable of optimizing these ranking factors, thereby elevating the visibility and impact of your videos.

As we forge ahead, we find ourselves delving into the rich tapestry of audience behavior patterns, a critical aspect that demands understanding for effective content scheduling. AI emerges as a beacon, offering insights into audience behavior data, and guiding creators in identifying scheduling patterns that hit the mark. This segment promises to unravel how AI ensures your content finds its viewers at the opportune moment, a strategy grounded in a deep understanding of audience consumption patterns.

As we venture further, we will unveil the strategies that stand to revolutionize content scheduling, offering a fresh perspective on leveraging AI to enhance content performance. This involves a deep dive into the nuances of audience behavior, a journey that promises to offer creators a roadmap to scheduling content that resonates with viewers, fostering engagement and building a loyal audience base.

As we progress in this chapter, we venture into the realm of AI-powered scheduling strategies, a domain where AI algorithms work tirelessly, analyzing a plethora of data to pinpoint the optimal moments for content release, thereby promising enhanced engagement and reach.

First on the agenda is the discussion on content timing optimization algorithms, a cornerstone in AI-powered scheduling strategies. These sophisticated algorithms sift through a vast array of data encompassing audience behavior, demographics, and historical context, to carve out the most opportune time slots for your content release. Here, we will unravel the mechanics of these AI-driven algorithms, shedding light on how they can be leveraged to fine-tune scheduling strategies, enhancing the potential reach and impact of your YouTube videos.

As we steer forward, we find ourselves amidst a rich discussion on the myriad factors that influence content release timing. AI stands as a powerful tool, capable of considering a wide spectrum of elements including audience engagement patterns, time zones, and the relevance of topics, all to optimize the release timing of content. This segment promises to offer a deep understanding of the critical factors that AI algorithms prioritize in determining the ideal release schedule, a strategy grounded in a meticulous analysis of diverse data points.

Navigating further, we reach the juncture where data-driven insights become the focal point, offering a roadmap to making informed scheduling decisions. AI emerges as a reliable ally, offering insights gleaned from analyzing audience behavior, identifying peak engagement times, and tracking content demand trends. In this part of our journey, we will elucidate how AI-driven tools harness these insights, guiding creators in making informed decisions on the release timing of videos, a strategy designed to maximize impact and reach.

As we draw this segment to a close, we stand with a rich understanding of AI-powered scheduling strategies, a domain where AI algorithms work in harmony with creators, offering data-driven insights and optimization strategies designed to enhance content reach and engagement. Through a meticulous exploration of AI's role in optimizing content scheduling, we aim to offer creators a blueprint for success, a strategy grounded in intelligence, analysis, and precision. This chapter promises to be a rich resource, offering creators a pathway to navigate the complex landscape of YouTube content scheduling with AI as a trusted guide, steering towards success with data-backed strategies and insights. Let us forge ahead, as we continue to unravel the transformative potential of AI in YouTube content scheduling, a journey promising enhanced reach, engagement, and success in the competitive YouTube arena.

In the dynamic world of YouTube content creation, the timing of content release stands as a pivotal determinant of a video's success. As we proceed in this chapter, we will unravel the intricacies of AI-driven content scheduling, a strategy grounded in intelligence and precision, promising creators a pathway to enhanced reach and engagement.

Embarking on this journey, we first turn our attention to smart analytics for content performance analysis, a domain where AI-driven tools stand as powerful allies, offering in-depth insights into key performance metrics including view counts, watch time, and audience engagement. Here, we will delve into the functionalities of these AI-powered analytics, elucidating how they can guide creators in optimizing content scheduling, a strategy designed to foster data-driven decision-making.

As we navigate further, we find ourselves amidst a rich discussion on identifying trends and viewer preferences, a task significantly enhanced by AI algorithms capable of discerning patterns in viewer behavior and content consumption. In this segment, we will shed light on how AI can aid creators in aligning content scheduling with viewer preferences, a strategy promising increased viewership and engagement.

Venturing ahead, we reach the realm of real-time optimization and adaptive scheduling, where AI emerges as a reliable guide, offering insights as performance metrics unfold. Here, we will discuss how AI can aid creators in adapting scheduling strategies in real time, ensuring content is released at the most opportune moments, a strategy grounded in timely analysis and adaptation.

As we transition into the discussion on AI-enhanced automation and scheduling tools, we find ourselves exploring AI-driven content scheduling platforms, tools designed to automate the scheduling process, taking into account a plethora of factors including audience behavior and channel analytics. In this segment, we will elucidate how AI can streamline the content release workflow, promising optimal timing and enhanced efficiency.

Further, we delve into the functionalities of AI in automating publishing and distribution strategies, a domain where AI stands as a powerful ally, managing content distribution across various platforms and social media channels. Here, we will discuss how AI can save creators time and effort, offering automated solutions grounded in intelligence and precision.

As we steer towards the end of this segment, we find ourselves amidst a discussion on predictive analytics for scheduling optimization, a domain where AI-based predictive analytics hold the potential to forecast future trends and audience engagement patterns. Here, we will unravel the potential of predictive analytics in optimizing content scheduling, offering insights into the best times for content release, a strategy designed to maximize impact and reach.

As we approach the conclusion of this chapter, we venture into the discussion on collaboration and adaptation in scheduling strategies, a domain where collaboration between AI and human creators stands central. Here, we will discuss how creators can work hand-in-hand with AI, leveraging insights while also applying creative intuition, a strategy promising a harmonious blend of technology and creativity.

In conclusion, we stand with a rich understanding of AI-driven content scheduling, a strategy promising enhanced reach and engagement. Through a meticulous exploration of AI's role in content scheduling, we aim to offer creators a blueprint for success, a strategy grounded in data-driven insights and automation. Join us as we embrace the transformative potential of AI in content scheduling, a journey promising enhanced reach, engagement, and success in the competitive YouTube arena.

Chapter 20
AI for Collaborative Projects

In this chapter, we will explore the power of AI in collaborative projects, focusing on its ability to enhance content creation, streamline workflows, improve team coordination, and optimize productivity. We will discuss the benefits of collaboration in content creation, the challenges and limitations it presents, and how AI can be leveraged to overcome these challenges and maximize the potential of collaborative efforts.

Collaboration is at the core of content creation, enabling diverse perspectives, expertise, and creativity to come together to produce high-quality work. We will discuss the importance of collaboration in generating innovative and engaging content, fostering synergy among team members, and enhancing the overall quality of the end result. AI can enhance collaborative projects by providing tools and technologies that support seamless communication, efficient task allocation, and effective feedback mechanisms.

Although collaboration brings numerous benefits, it also presents challenges and limitations that can hinder the progress and effectiveness of collaborative projects. We will explore common challenges such as communication barriers, coordination issues, and productivity gaps, and discuss how AI can help address these challenges through automated workflows, intelligent task allocation, and real-time performance monitoring.

AI technologies offer immense potential for enhancing collaboration in content creation. We will delve into how AI algorithms and tools can augment team coordination, automate repetitive tasks, provide real-time feedback, and optimize productivity. By leveraging AI, teams can overcome collaboration challenges, streamline their workflows, and achieve greater efficiency and effectiveness in their projects.

Effective project management is critical for successful collaboration. We will explore how AI-powered project management tools can automate task allocation, track progress, and enhance team coordination. These tools can leverage AI algorithms to analyze project requirements, team capabilities, and resource availability, enabling efficient task assignment and prioritization.

Collaborative editing is a fundamental aspect of content creation. We will discuss how AI can facilitate real-time collaboration, allowing team members to work on the same document simultaneously, provide instant feedback, and track changes efficiently. AI-driven tools can enable seamless collaboration by automating version control, resolving conflicts, and improving overall editing efficiency.

Effective communication is vital for successful collaboration. We will explore how AI can enhance communication and feedback mechanisms through intelligent chatbots, natural language processing, and sentiment analysis. AI-powered communication tools can facilitate seamless and efficient interactions among team members, enable real-time feedback, and enhance overall project communication.

Assigning tasks and prioritizing them efficiently is crucial for collaboration. We will discuss how AI algorithms can analyze project requirements, team skills and availability, and resource constraints to intelligently allocate tasks. AI-driven task assignment and prioritization can optimize team productivity, ensure balanced workloads, and enhance overall project efficiency.

Coordinating team activities, scheduling meetings, and managing deadlines can be challenging in collaborative projects. We will explore how AI can automate team coordination and scheduling tasks by analyzing team calendars, availability, and project milestones. AI-powered coordination and scheduling tools can minimize scheduling conflicts, improve meeting efficiency, and ensure timely task completion.

Monitoring team productivity and analyzing individual performance are essential for project success. We will discuss how AI algorithms can track team activities, analyze productivity metrics, and provide real-time performance feedback. AI-driven productivity monitoring and performance analysis tools can identify bottlenecks, optimize resource allocation, and help teams continuously improve their collaboration and productivity.

Creating content collaboratively requires effective teamwork and seamless content integration. We will explore how AI can assist in joint content creation by analyzing team inputs, providing content suggestions, and facilitating content merging and integration. AI-powered content creation tools can enhance collaboration, improve content quality, and accelerate the creative process.

Editing is a critical phase in content creation that often requires collaboration and iterative feedback. We will discuss how AI can provide real-time feedback during the editing process, offering suggestions for improvement, identifying errors, and enhancing overall content quality. AI-powered editing assistance can streamline the editing workflow, reduce errors, and optimize content iteration.

Version control and content iteration are essential for collaborative projects, ensuring that everyone is working on the most up-to-date and aligned content. We will explore how AI can enhance version control and content iteration by automating conflict resolution, tracking changes, and enabling seamless content integration. AI-driven version control can minimize content conflicts, simplify content merging, and facilitate efficient collaboration.

Data analysis plays a crucial role in effective decision making. We will discuss how AI algorithms can analyze large volumes of data, extract meaningful insights, and provide data-driven recommendations. AI-powered data analysis can enable collaborative decision making by providing teams with valuable insights into audience preferences, content performance, and market trends.

Opinions and feedback from team members are valuable inputs for collaborative decision making. We will explore how AI can assist in opinion mining by analyzing team feedback, sentiment analysis, and consensus building. AI-powered opinion mining tools can help teams aggregate and understand diverse opinions, identify consensus points, and facilitate decision-making processes.

Ethics and responsible decision making are crucial aspects of collaborative projects. We will explore the ethical considerations surrounding AI-enabled decision making, such as ensuring fairness, transparency, and accountability. AI-based decision-making tools should be designed and utilized ethically to align with legal and moral standards, protecting individual rights and fostering a collaborative and inclusive environment.

In global collaborative projects, language barriers can hinder communication and collaboration. We will discuss how AI can enable cross-language communication and translation by providing real-time translation and transcription services. AI-powered language translation tools can facilitate seamless communication among team members from different linguistic backgrounds, enabling effective collaboration.

Virtual collaboration tools and virtual reality (VR) environments have emerged as valuable resources for remote team collaboration. We will explore how AI can enhance virtual collaboration by providing interactive and immersive experiences, facilitating real-time communication, and enabling synchronized virtual workspaces. AI-driven virtual collaboration tools can bridge the gap between remote team members, fostering a sense of presence and enhancing collaborative engagement.

Cultural sensitivity and inclusivity are critical in global collaborative projects that involve diverse teams from different cultural backgrounds. We will discuss how AI can assist in promoting cultural sensitivity by providing guidelines, cultural insights, and translation services. AI-driven cultural sensitivity tools can help teams maintain respect for diverse cultural practices, promote inclusivity, and foster a positive and collaborative working environment.

Evaluating project progress and quality is essential for maintaining project standards. We will explore how AI algorithms can automate project evaluation by analyzing project metrics, performance indicators, and benchmarks. AI-driven project evaluation tools can provide objective insights, identify areas for improvement, and enhance overall project quality.

Quality control ensures that the deliverables meet the expected standards and requirements. We will discuss how AI can assist in quality control and performance analysis by automating quality checks, analyzing data, and providing real-time feedback. AI-powered quality control tools can minimize errors, enhance content quality, and improve overall project performance.

Continuous improvement and iteration are fundamental to successful collaborative projects. We will explore how AI can support continuous improvement by analyzing project data, identifying improvement areas, and facilitating project iteration. AI algorithms can provide insights for process optimization, identify bottlenecks, and help teams iteratively enhance their collaboration and project outcomes.

Collaboration in content publishing and distribution is essential for ensuring content reaches the right audience effectively. We will discuss how AI can enable collaborative content publishing and distribution by automating content scheduling, streamlining distribution processes, and optimizing content placement. AI-driven collaborative tools can enhance teamwork, increase content visibility, and maximize audience reach.

Promoting and marketing content require effective collaboration to ensure maximum exposure. We will explore how AI can assist in content promotion and marketing by analyzing audience preferences, recommending promotional channels, and optimizing marketing strategies. AI-powered content promotion tools can augment collaborative efforts, target the right audiences, and enhance content visibility and discoverability.

Audience engagement and feedback are invaluable for content creators. We will discuss how AI can assist in enhancing audience engagement and gathering feedback by analyzing audience behavior, sentiment analysis, and interactive features. AI-powered audience engagement tools can foster collaborative interactions, improve user experience, and facilitate meaningful feedback that enables creators to fine-tune their content.

Protecting intellectual property and detecting plagiarism are essential in collaborative projects. We will explore how AI algorithms can analyze content databases, detect copyright infringement, and identify potential instances of plagiarism. AI-powered copyright and plagiarism detection tools can safeguard intellectual property, promote fairness, and ensure responsible collaboration among team members.

Secure collaboration platforms are vital for protecting sensitive information and maintaining data integrity. We will discuss how AI can enhance collaboration security by providing encryption, authentication, and access control mechanisms. AI-driven secure collaboration platforms can ensure data privacy, protect intellectual property, and facilitate secure information exchange among team members.

Ethics and responsible collaboration are essential considerations in AI-driven collaborative projects. We will discuss the importance of ethical AI practices, such as fairness, transparency, and accountability, in safeguarding collaboration integrity and protecting individual rights. Ethical and responsible collaboration with AI ensures that team members are treated equitably, data privacy is preserved, and intellectual property rights are respected.

AI technology is rapidly advancing, opening new possibilities for collaboration in diverse industries. We will explore the future advancements in AI-driven collaboration tools and platforms, such as enhanced coordination, intelligent automation, and augmented decision making. The future holds immense potential for AI-enabled collaboration, enabling teams to achieve higher levels of productivity, efficiency, and innovation.

Emerging AI technologies offer exciting prospects for collaboration in content creation. We will discuss emerging AI technologies, such as natural language processing, computer vision, and deep learning, and their potential to revolutionize content collaboration. These technologies can facilitate seamless communication, automate complex tasks, and unlock new creative possibilities for teams.

AI-driven collaboration tools and platforms have the potential to revolutionize and enhance collaborative projects in various industries, including content creation. By leveraging AI algorithms and technologies, teams can improve coordination, streamline workflows, and enhance overall productivity. The future holds even more promising advancements in AI-enabled collaboration, making it easier for teams to achieve their goals and deliver high-quality content. Join us as we explore the power of AI for collaborative projects and discover the limitless possibilities it brings to the world of content creation.

The FUTURE of YOUTUBE

Jeremy Schreifels

A versatile creative force, educator, and entrepreneurial guide. With a foundation in drumming and a air for songwriting, he seamlessly transitioned into international music production, crafting harmonious blends that bridge cultures. Jeremy's journey extended into authorship, where his words inspire and enlighten. A seasoned coach, he empowers entrepreneurs to channel creativity into business success. Jeremy's milestones, from performing with renowned musicians to coaching business owners, reect his dedication to integrity, passion, and the boundless possibilities of the creative spirit.

Aaron Gear

Not just a name, but a brand synonymous with versatility, innovation, and leadership in multiple industries. With a rich background that spans the entertainment industry, business, law enforcement, marketing, and government contracting, Aaron's expertise is both broad and deep. His journey in the entertainment sector, particularly in set and prop design construction, has given him unique insights that he often shares through his insightful blogs. These writings, which also cover topics like business, law enforcement, marketing, and inuence, have become a source of inspiration for many.